CHARLES J. HAUGHEY

KINSALEY

TADHG KENNEDY

Atlantic Press
Dublin
1986

FIRST EDITION
April 1986

© 1986 Tadhg Kennedy

ISBN 0 9509727 2 X (Paperback)

ISBN 0 9509727 I I (Hardback)

Cover Design by: Fionan O'Connell.

Printed by: Future Print, Baldoyle, Dublin 13.

Published by: Atlantic Press, 124 Strand Road, Portmarnock, Co. Dublin, Ireland.

For

Nuncy

Dearbhail and Donnchadh

ACKNOWLEDGMENTS

The author wishes to acknowledge and to express his gratitude to all who contributed in any way to the compilation and successful completion of this book. Many people gave generously of their time and knowledge and I am greatly indebted to them. Particular thanks to Charles Haughey, his family and the staffs at Abbeville, Leinster House and Mount Street; Fionan O'Connell, photographer; Noel G. Flanagan, author and historian; David Leahy, artist; John Kennedy, Bridget Kennedy, Helen Leahy, Nuala, Catherine, Niamh and Sinead, Independent Newspapers, Irish Press, Irish Times, Sunday World, Sunday Tribune, Magill Magazine, The Phoenix, The Directors and Staffs of The Gilbert Library, The National Library, Public Records Office, Registry of Deeds and Wills, Royal Irish Academy, Clonliffe Diocesan Library, Ordnance Survey Phoenix Park, Malahide, Raheny and Pearse Street Public Libraries.

I was unable to ascertain ownership of some photographs. I would be grateful if the owners would contact me, in order to give them their rightful acknowledgement in future impressions.

124 Strand Road   **Tadhg Kennedy**
Portmarnock   **April 1986**
Co. Dublin

CONTENTS

Chapter 1

ABBEVILLE

Abbeville, Kinsaley was built for the Right Honourable John Beresford, brother of the 1st Marquess of Waterford. Beresford served as First Commissioner but he was actually the most powerful man in Ireland at the end of the 18th century. It was he who once stated that no Lord Lieutenant in Ireland could exist without his power. He was also described by Lord Fitzwilliam as "King of Ireland". Prior to Beresford's time, a house stood on the same location at Kinsaley.It was marked on early maps as "Abbeywell". Before 1820, the name was changed to Abbeville in honour of a young girl from the village of Abbeville in Northern France, who became its new mistress. The new additions to the original house were designed by James Gandon, the famous architect and friend of Beresford. Gandon was responsible for many of the most beautiful neo-classical buildings in Dublin. The Four Courts and the Custom House are fine examples of his work.

Gandon's work on Abbeville is exquisite and rare. Viewed from the front driveway, the house looks deceptively small. The four baseless Doric columns at the entrance door are in the style of the ancient Greek. Gandon consistently preferred Roman architecture and his work may be styled "neo-classical". The entrance to Abbeville represents a rare departure from the neo-classical in a long life of over 80 years. Immediately inside the front door, one is confronted with a magnificent flight of wide stone steps. The reception rooms are beautifully hung with many original paintings and ancient maps, while rare books on history and the arts adorn the bookshelves. There are many volumes on horses, the great sporting love of the present owners, the Haughey family. The head of the family is the famous politician of international repute, Charles James Haughey, known to everybody as "Charlie".

Front entrance to Abbeville. There is an imposing flight of stone steps immediately inside the door. *(Photo: Fionan O'Connell.)*

Emsworth, Kinsaley was designed by Gandon in 1794 for James Woodmason. It is the outstanding example of a villa built entirely to Gandon's specifications. *(Photo: Courtesy G. L. McGuinness Collection.)*

The most exquisitely decorated room in the house, is the ballroom. This spacious room is divided in three by two low-slung segmental arches. The ceiling is of Adamesque plasterwork with husk decoration on the walls which incorporates circular painted medallions. McParland, the expert on Gandon's work, states that the ballroom in Abbeville is the most splendid and least known example of Irish neo-classical domestic interiors in existence. (*Vitruvius Hibernicus,* London, 1985). Gandon also added a dairy and stables at Abbeville. The dairy is more delicately refined and McParland refers to it as one of Gandon's prettiest drawings. He goes on to say that the dry rectilinear elegance of the Abbeville stables and dairy, display an architectural power unique at the time among Irish architects. The original Abbeville House was built in the Elizabethan style. It was so beautiful that Gandon decided to leave the best of it and build around it. This he accomplished very successfully. Gandon worked on Abbeville at various times between 1763 and 1790. He died in 1823 at the age of 81 years.

An extract from the book, *"Beauties of Ireland"*, reads: "Adjoining Greenwood is Abbeville, a fine mansion, with extensive gardens and plantations. The house was principally erected by Right Hon. John Beresford, after the designs of Mr. Gandon, architect of the Custom House, Dublin. The gardens are perhaps the most extensive and the best arranged of any, in the vicinity of the metropolis. This place afforded an occasional summer residence to several of the lords lieutenant of Ireland, previous to the acquisition by government of the vice-regal lodge in the Phoenix Park". The vice-regal lodge is now known as, "Aras an Uachtarain" and serves as the official residence of the President of Ireland.

John Beresford passed away in 1805 and Abbeville was inherited by his son John Claudius, the banker. Just ten years later, Austin Cooper F.S.A. became the new owner of Abbeville. Cooper was a famous and meticulous 18th century antiquarian. His writings survive in a book entitled, *"An 18th Century Antiquary 1759-1830"*. He describes his arrival on Tuesday, 15 August, 1815 and on the following Saturday, 19 August, Cooper writes that the "Kingsaly tenants had a bonfire to celebrate occasion coming to Abbeville with Musick etc.".

BERESFORD

ARMS:
Quarterly, 1st and 4th, arg. semée of cross crosslets fitchée and three fleurs-de-lis, a bordure engrailed sa. Beresford. 2nd and 3d arg. a chief indented sa. De la Poer.

CREST:
A dragon's head erased az. pierced through the neck with a broken tilting spear or. the broken point arg. in the mouth. Beresford. A stag's head cabossed ppr. attired or. between the horns a crucifix of the last. De La Poer.

SUPPORTERS:
Two angels ppr. vested arg. crined and winged or. each holding in the exterior hand a sword erect also ppr.

MOTTO:
Nil nisi cruce.

Austin Cooper was the great great grandson of an Austin Cooper who left Surrey in England and settled in Blessington, County Wicklow. Known as Austin the Settler, he became famous for his unusual feats of strength. A favourite trick of his was to lift two men, one in each hand, slap them together and throw them on a dunghill. In contrast, his great great grandson Austin Cooper F.S.A. was an academic who loved to investigate old buildings, churches and graveyards. He was born at Killenure near Dundrum, County Tipperary in February 1752. He was employed by the Treasury Office and he was appointed Deputy Constable of Dublin Castle in 1796. He also managed the properties of several noblemen and he became a wealthy man. He had a fine family vault built at the ruined church of St. Nicholas, Kinsaley. The vault is still in a perfect state of preservation. In 1830, while on his way from Kinsaley to Dublin, Cooper was involved in a tragic carriage accident. Early 19th century roads were in an appalling state. Hely Dutton in 1802 wrote:

"We see round smooth stones as large as a man's head, rolling about the road and the sand flying in clouds with the least breath of wind. Large round stones and sand can never sink equally under the pressure of heavy wheels and from their shape, round stones cannot remain firm, for every time a wheel stirs them in dry weather, the sand steals under them, and at length they are thrown out on the road, where they roll about, laming horses and breaking the springs of carriages, until stopped by the ditch, or are scraped off in the mud. I have observed roads covered a foot deep at once with wet strand mud and large round stones mixed; such a body of so soft a material, laid on at once, is after the first rains converted into puddle, and scraped off, and thrown into heaps; then a fresh supply of the same mud is laid on, and the same process continued. Nothing ruins roads so much as permitting mud to accumulate on the surface; on many roads it is upwards of six inches deep; no road, let it be ever so well constructed or made, can stand this great neglect."

As a result of his injuries when the carriage overturned, Austin Cooper died shortly afterwards on 30 August, 1830. Cooper left a huge personal collection of rare works. He owned a copy of Archdall's *"Monasticon Hibernicum"* and the second book of the

(Drawn by David Leahy)

COOPER.

ARMS:
Sa. a chevron wavy erm. between three lions rampant or.

CREST:
On a chapeau gu. turned up erm. a bull passant ppr. collared and hoofed or.

MOTTO:
Love Serve.

7

"Annals of the Four Masters," *1171-1616.* O'Donovan based his edition of the "Four Masters" on this manuscript.

Soon after the death of Austin Cooper, Abbeville was sold to Professor James William Cusack M.D. and Surgeon-in-Ordinary to the Crown in Ireland. He invited his brother Samuel and his family to come and live at Abbeville after the death of his wife. Doctor Samuel Cusack had two children, a boy and girl. The eldest child, Margaret Anna was to become internationally famous and is known to history as, "The Nun of Kenmare". After her parents separated, Margaret Anna went to live in England with her mother. Some time later when her fiancé died of a fever, she became an Anglican nun. Soon after, she became a convert to Catholicism and she joined the Sisters of Penance for a short time. In 1859 she moved to Newry, County Down where she joined the Irish Poor Clare Nuns. Some time later she opened a convent in Kenmare, County Kerry where she worked on behalf of the poor. It was in Kenmare that she wrote most of her 50 books. She took a keen interest in history and politics and it was highly unusual at the time for a Poor Clare Nun to publish books. Later she resided at Knock, County Mayo and she expressed some doubts about the Apparition there. She discovered that Father Cavanagh's housekeeper liked a drink and was accustomed to seeing wonderful things. The housekeeper is credited with being one of the first people to see the Apparition at Knock. Margaret Anna, now known as Sister Mary Francis Clare, went to Rome in 1884. She obtained permission from Pope Leo XIII to found the Order of The Sisters of Saint Joseph of Peace. She encountered great opposition from the Catholic clergy. Eventually she resigned from her Order and from the Catholic Church. After trying different Protestant Churches, she again became an Anglican. She died on 5 June 1899 at the age of 70 years. It was only in 1974 that Mother Francis Clare was officially recognised as the Foundress of the Sisters of Peace.

Professor James William Cusack died in 1861 and was succeeded by his eldest son, Henry Thomas Cusack. Henry T. died in 1865 and was succeeded by his eldest son, Athanasius Francis William Geoffrey de Geneville Cusack who was born at Florence in 1855. A. F. W. F. de G. Cusack was High Sheriff of County Dublin in 1881 and he died unmarried in 1887. He was succeeded by his younger

CUSACK

ARMS:
Per pale or. and az. a fess counterchanged, quartering Golding, St. Laurence, Beaufort, Holland and Plantagenet.

CREST:
A mermaid sa. holding in the dexter hand a sword, sinister, a sceptre.

MOTTOES:

Ave Maria, plena gratia.	Hail Mary, full of grace.
En Dieu est mon espoir.	In God is my hope.

9

brother, Major James William Henry Claud Cusack who was born at Lucca Baths in 1856. In 1887, he married his cousin, Mary Cusack of Furry Park, Raheny, Co. Dublin. He was High Sheriff in 1900 and he died without issue in 1929. He was succeeded by his cousin, Major Ralph Smith Oliver Cusack who was born in 1875. Although married twice, he died without issue in 1965 at the grand age of 90 years.

Abbeville was sold by Major R.S.O. Cusack to Percy Reynolds of C.I.E., the well known horse breeder. Reynolds sold the House and lands to Franz Zielkowski who managed the property for a brief period in the sixties.

In 1969, Abbeville came into the possession of an exciting, distinguished and controversial new owner. He may yet be recorded as the most important 20th century Irishman to have walked the stage of modern Irish history. A man born to be a leader. A man of vision and of great compassion for his native country and its citizens; a man who has truly understood the plight of the less fortunate in society, who has fearlessly defended the poor and the aged and who has worked unceasingly to improve their lot. He is a man who has endeavoured to re-awaken our pride in being natives of the green and ancient land of Eire; who continues to defend the traditional neutral role of Ireland and who has already carved for himself an exalted place among the world's leaders. Yes, who other than Charles J. Haughey.

Charles James Haughey was born in Castlebar, Co. Mayo on 16 September 1925. His mother was Sarah McWilliams and his father was Seán Haughey from Swatragh, Co. Derry. Seán Haughey was an Army Commandant in Castlebar when his son Charles was born. Shortly afterwards the whole family moved to Dublin. Charles was one of seven children, four boys and three girls. They are Pádraig, Seán, Eoghan, Bridie, Maureen and Eithne. Seán Haughey died on 3 January 1947. His wife, Sarah, is happily still with us. She has lived to see her children's successes and to enjoy the years that saw her son Charles become leader of Fianna Fail and Taoiseach of Ireland.

While a young student, Charles Haughey spent many a happy holiday with his relatives in Swatragh. He attended Scoil Mhuire Primary School in Marino and later went to St. Josephs C.B.S. in Fairview. Many famous people passed through Joey's, Fairview,

HAUGHEY.

ARMS:
Per pale or. and gu., a lion and stag all counterchanged, respecting each other. Dexter, the lion gu. rampant, supporting in the paws, a sword arg. erect. Sinister the stag or. rampant, supporting in the hoofs, a fasces arg. erect. Surmounted by a helmet ppr. inclining to profile with mantling gu. turned up arg.

CREST:
An antique crown or. A demi-horse arg. rampant, issuant out of the crown.

MOTTO:
Marte nostro.
By endeavour.

The heraldic shield represents the three main interests of Charles Haughey. The lion with sword represents the army. The stag with fasces represents the law and politics and the horse represents a lifelong interest in a favourite animal.

11

but the young Haughey was destined to be the most famous of all. Charles Haughey was a bright pupil who excelled at mathematics and languages. He found study easy and didn't have to spend long hours at it. From a young age he showed an excellent power of concentration. He was also a good mixer and a fearless sportsman. Football was his favourite game. He played usually in the half forward position for Joeys and later for Parnells. He continued his studies at University College Dublin, where he was regarded as a particularly brilliant academic. He joined Fianna Fail and graduated from U.C.D.with a Batchelor of Commerce degree. He read Law at the King's Inns and became a Barrister-at-Law. He is also a Fellow of the Institute of Chartered Accountants in Ireland. His first class qualifications cannot be matched in Dail Eireann. He was a Commissioned Officer of An Forsa Cosanta Aitiúil (F.C.A.) from 1947 to 1957.

On 18 September 1951, he married Maureen, the eldest daughter of Kathleen and Sean Lemass the former 1916 veteran and founder member of Fianna Fail. Four children were born to them. The eldest is their daughter Eimear who was born on 28 February 1955. Eimear loves horses and the outdoor life. She is currently the successful manager of Abbeville Stud. The second child is a son, Conor, who was born on 23 November 1957. Conor is a mining engineer and he is also a great lover of the outdoor life. His favourite sport is deep sea diving. The third child is a son, Ciaran, who was born on 23 June 1960. He is a keen business man who runs the Celtic Helicopter firm. Among other business interests, he has a share in a trendy Ely Place night club called Faces, which was opened in November 1985. The youngest child Seán was born on 8 November 1961. The year of 1985 was a memorable one for him. In June of that year and on his first attempt, he was elected an Alderman of Dublin Corporation in the Local Elections. He represents Artane. The four seater Artane electoral district had a total valid poll of 13,285. The quota was 2,658. Seán Haughey received 3,956 first preference votes and was the only candidate out of 15 contenders to be elected on the first count. It was a remarkable achievement for a young man of 23 years. On Thursday 14 November 1985, Seán was conferred with a Batchelor of Arts degree at Trinity College, Dublin.

Wedding Day. Charles Haughey and Maureen Lemass were married on 18 September 1951. *(Photo: Courtesy Irish Press.)*

At Grangemore, Raheny in North County Dublin.
L. to r. Ciaran, Maureen, Eimear on the pony holding Sean and Conor nearby.*(Photo: Courtesy Independent Newspapers.)*

14

L. to r. Sean, Conor, Charles, Eimear, Ciaran and Maureen.

Charles and Maureen with their young family.

(*Photo: Courtesy Irish Times.*)

Maureen Haughey was born the eldest daughter of Seán and Kathleen Lemass. Seán Lemass was the noted Taoiseach of Ireland who brought the country from a dependence on agriculture straight into the industrial age. His life and work are well documented and it would take an entire book to do justice to the story of his life and achievements. Seán and Kathleen were an ideal couple, each one complementing the other. Seán was serious minded while Kathleen pursued her keen interest in the arts and music. She won many prizes at Feiseanna Cheoil. They virtually grew up together as their families were friends. When Seán went to prison after the Civil War, Kathleen corresponded regularly with him. When Seán was released from prison, they decided to marry. They had three daughters and one son. They were Mrs. Maureen Haughey, Mrs. Sheila O'Connor, Mrs. Peggy Ui Bhriain and Noel who subsequently became a T.D. for Dublin South West and who died in 1976. Sean Lemass died in 1971 and his wife lived on to the grand old age of 87 years. She died on Thursday 14 March 1985. In a special statement, Charles Haughey spoke of his mother-in-law in the following terms:

"Mrs Lemass was a very exceptional person. She was totally devoted to her husband and her family and dedicated her whole life to looking after them and providing the support and encouragement which are needed by people in public life.

"She was kind and gracious and totally unselfish. She always wanted to see the best in everybody and I doubt if she ever said a bad word about anybody in her whole life, no matter how great the temptation to do so.

"She was very much part of an old Dublin way of life, which was home-based and in which amusement and entertainment were provided within the family circle with great emphasis on, and a love of, music in particular. She had a long and fulfilling life, dedicated to others and their needs and problems, and she is certainly gone straight to the reward in heaven for which she worked and prayed all her life."

Maureen inherited many of her parents' attributes. She foresook her academic and political interests to concentrate on her domestic responsibilities. While her husband was building up his business interests and his political career, Maureen took good care of her young family. She reared one daughter and three sons and being a

Sean and Kathleen Lemass at home.   *(Photo: Courtesy Irish Times.)*

typical good mother, she has no complaints to make about any of them. She is used to the rough and tumble of political life in Ireland. She has the unique distinction of being the daughter of a Taoiseach and the wife of a Taoiseach. Maureen Haughey is above all, a homemaker. She knows only too well, the severe demands that are made on a politician, the unforeseen disruptions of holiday plans, the long meetings, the anxieties and the tiredness. In her own quiet and kind way, she has devoted herself to looking after her husband and family. Like her family, she is a lover of the outdoor life. Her favourite interests are horse riding and horse racing. She is also a breeder of Irish Wolfhounds. Reading is a favourite indoor pastime, in particular books on historical subjects.

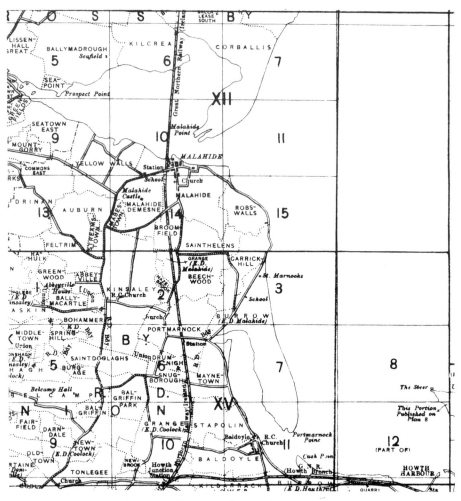

The Kinsaley area from the Townland Index of County Dublin. (Based on the Ordnance Survey by permission of the Government. Permit No. 4597.)

CHAPTER 2

THE SIXTIES AND SEVENTIES

Charles Haughey was a member of Fianna Fail since his student days. It was after his marriage to Maureen that he began to seriously work towards a seat in Dail Eireann. He built up his support in contesting three elections. In the General Election of March 1957 he was elected for the first time to the Dail. Harry Colley, father of the late George Colley T.D., was the defeated Fianna Fail candidate. From his election in '57, Charles Haughey T.D. was never to lose his seat in the Dail. In fact he has constantly and consistently achieved one of the highest first preference votes in general elections.

During this time he was building up his accountancy firm. Through initiative and hard work the firm and C.J. prospered. After only three years in the Dail, Charles Haughey showed such an ability and knowledge of administration that on 6 May 1960 he was appointed Parliamentary Secretary to the Minister for Justice, Oscar Traynor. One year later Traynor retired and Charles Haughey became Minister for Justice on 11 October 1961.

He was noted among his subordinates as a tough but able and liberal minister. He carried out far-reaching reforms and he put many new bills successfully through the Dail. He brought into being the Civil Liability Act, the Succession Act, the Criminal Justice Legal Aid Act among others. He provided a special detention centre for young offenders. Up to that time they had to serve their sentences in adult prisons. He abolished the death penalty by hanging except for a few categories of murder. He changed the law in order to guarantee widows one third of their husband's property. He was a very capable, very efficient and very hardworking minister whose dominant features were his humanity and compassion for the needy.

After the dramatic resignation of Paddy Smith, Minister for Agriculture, Sean Lemass appointed Charles Haughey to take over

The four Taoisigh and Leaders of Fianna Fail. Eamonn De Valera (f. 4th from left); Sean Lemass (f. 3rd from left); Jack Lynch (b. 2nd from left); Charles Haughey (b. 4th from left).

in his place. On the 8th of November 1964, the new Minister for Agriculture took up his post. It was a time of much agitation among farmers. However, the quick, accurate and thorough grasp of his portfolio meant that Charles Haughey made some outstanding improvements in the whole area of agriculture. He saw with compassion, the poverty of families on small holdings in the West of Ireland. He devised an income supplement which allowed them to raise their level of subsistence a little above the poverty margin. In the short two years he spent in Agriculture and by sheer ability, he accomplished an enormous amount of work. He set the scene for a reformation and growth in farming which has continued down to the present day.

After the 1965 General Election, Fianna Fail won 72 seats and formed a new administration under Sean Lemass. Lemass retired in 1966 and the two main contenders for Taoiseach and Leader of Fianna Fail were Charles Haughey and George Colley. Lemass requested both men to retire from the contest in favour of an agreed candidate, Jack Lynch. Charles Haughey withdrew his name but Colley would not. Lynch won easily. On 16 November 1966, Charles Haughey was appointed Minister for Finance. He was the ablest man in the Dail for the job and it has to be recognised in retrospect, that he was the most successful Finance Minister in modern times.

Charles Haughey always had a compassionate and genuine concern for people in difficulty. As Minister for Finance he introduced many innovative and profound changes in Irish society. He gave old age pensioners free electricity, free radio and television licences. He also granted them free travel on public transport. Disabled motorists were granted free petrol in 1969 and in his budget of 1970 he introduced a deserted wives allowance for the first time. A really innovative piece of legislation was the exemption from income tax of creative writers and artists. It recalls a time in ancient Ireland when, "Na Fili" or the old Celtic Bards, story tellers and musicians went untaxed and were even fed and housed by the ancient Irish chieftains. The soul of a nation is encapsulated by its living artists and preserved for posterity. Charles Haughey had the vision to recognise this fact. His great compassion for the average person struggling to survive, is perhaps his greatest virtue. His frequent introduction of brave new legislation to improve their lot

With Senator Robert Kennedy in the sixties.

stands to his credit forever. He has a genuine feeling for the needs of people. In many instances he has brushed away harsh, convoluted laws and constraints and replaced them with modern more streamlined machinery geared to the needs of real people. The people in turn, have recognised him for his efforts and achievements. He is genuinely loved by those who know him best in his own constituency. At general elections he constantly and consistently achieves the highest first preference vote of any politician in Ireland. His career in Finance was to have a sudden and traumatic ending in early May 1970.

By August 1969, Charles Haughey was the most successful Minister for Finance since the formation of the Republic of Ireland. The economy boomed during his time. However, in that fateful month of August 1969, events in the Northern part of our country had a dramatic effect on his position. A concerted attack on the citizens of North-East Ireland took place. Whole streets of houses in some Catholic areas of Belfast were burnt out. Homeless and injured men, women and children began to pour South across the border. A new phase of killings and intimidation had begun. The Taoiseach, Jack Lynch was alleged to have stated that he would not stand idly by and let such atrocities continue unabated. Mobile military hospitals were set up along the border to treat victims of the violence. A cabinet committee was formed to develop contacts with the North-East sector. The Irish State also contributed about £100,000 for the relief of distress in North-East Ireland. The special cabinet committee was composed of Charles Haughey, Neil Blaney, Padraig Faulkner and Jim Gibbons. In April 1970, drama heightened. The Taoiseach, Jack Lynch was informed that a consignment of arms was due to arrive at Dublin airport.

Towards the end of April and in early May of 1970, there was much activity in the British embassy. The leader of the Opposition, Liam Cosgrave went to Jack Lynch and informed him that he had received a message which implied that a number of Fianna Fail ministers were involved in the importation of arms. For reasons that remain incomprehensible to the voting public, the source or sender of the message to Cosgrave has never been disclosed. Jack Lynch asked for the resignations of Neil Blaney and Charles Haughey. They refused. They were dismissed. The 7 May 1970 was his last day as Minister for Finance. He was wrongfully accused in what was to become known as the "Arms Trial".

Charles Haughey denied that he had anything to do with the illegal importation of arms, or had participated in any attempt to illegally import arms into Ireland. He further stated that he accepted the decision of the Taoiseach and leader of Fianna Fail. He unselfishly and magnanimously added that he believed that the unity of the Fianna Fail party was of greater importance to the welfare of the nation than was his political career.

Charles Haughey, Neil Blaney, Captain Kelly, John Kelly from Belfast and Albert Lukyx from Belgium were charged with attempting to import arms illegally. The case against Blaney was dismissed in the district court while the others were sent for trial to the Central Criminal Court. The jury found all defendants not guilty. The trial made sensational headlines and hundreds of column inches were written. Everyone had an opinion. Charles Haughey was now an international figure. His good name, integrity and reputation were completely vindicated. He had suffered a great injustice. He had lost his senior ministerial post and was vilified by many and yet he was not found guilty of any misdemeanour. It was surely a high price for anybody to pay. It is from this point onwards that the strength of character of Charles Haughey becomes evident. Blaney, Boland and Brennan resigned from Fianna Fail. Charles Haughey stayed with the Party. Fianna Fail entered a few years of delayed shock after 1970. They lost the 1973 general election. Charles Haughey was first to recover. He worked on steadily and encouraged his colleagues. On 3 August 1973 he became Chairman of the Joint Committee on the Secondary Legislation of the European Communities. He contributed greatly to the steadying of the Fianna Fail nerve. It was inevitable that he would be recalled to the front bench. In 1975 he was appointed Shadow Minister for Health.

In the General Election of 1977 Fianna Fail were back in government with a landslide victory of 84 seats, the highest number ever. Charles Haughey was appointed Minister for Health and Social Welfare on 5 July 1977. Again, he demonstrated his ability, industry and imagination.

24

The Haugheys and friends and a lifelong interest in horses.

25

He was to carry out the most far-reaching reforms in that Department since the foundation of the State. His ability to communicate with the public and the clergy coupled with his ability to push through new and innovative legislation, was limitless. He successfully guided important Legislation on contraception through the Dail at a time when it was unfashionable to do so. He worked hard and achieved much. While a Minister, he introduced campaigns for physical fitness and anti-smoking drives. He also organised the free distribution of toothbrushes for children. He generally raised the level of awareness of the population in regard to their health. His anti-smoking campaign created a national awareness of the now proven health risks attached to the inhalation of cigarette smoke. He was again to the fore in trying to prevent the citizens of Ireland from unwittingly causing untold damage to themselves. No matter what ministry he occupied, people and their needs were always his first priority. He would often cut through red tape and civil service mountains of paper to help those in need.

CHAPTER 3

TAOISEACH OF IRELAND

On 5 December 1979, Jack Lynch suddenly announced his resignation as Taoiseach and leader of Fianna Fail. Two days later the election for his successor took place. There were only two serious contenders for the position. They were Charles Haughey and George Colley. It appears that the outgoing Taoiseach and the majority of his cabinet favoured Colley. C.J. had his homework completed however. When it came to a vote, the result was Charles Haughey 44, George Colley 38. Charlie was Taoiseach after 22 years as a T.D. He had reached the pinnacle of his career.

On 7 December 1979 Dail Eireann voted Charles Haughey as Taoiseach of Ireland. No sooner had the new Taoiseach been elected than the Leader of the Opposition, Garret Fitzgerald, launched into a vitriolic and personal attack on Mr. Haughey, the like of which has seldom been heard in the Dail. When Fitzgerald was asked to elaborate on his reference to Charlie's "flawed pedigree", he simply stated that he could not say precisely what he meant. This silly and juvenile outburst was incomprehensible and contributed greatly to a subsequent loss of esteem for Fitzgerald. Journalists later said that, "the most nauseating spectacle the Dail has witnessed in decades was the scurrilous and mean attack on the person of Charles Haughey by Garret Fitzgerald. In a speech full of moral indignation and self-righteousness the new Taoiseach's character was blackened by a series of innuendo, half-truths and generalisations . . . Fitzgerald's performance demeaned him in the eyes of many who thought him a bigger and more gracious man". Unfortunately for Haughey, he was too human and too generous in his treatment of those who opposed him in Fianna Fail. It gave others the excuse to lable him an indecisive and unsure Taoiseach. It most likely encouraged his opponents to carry out bitter attacks on

The Taoiseach and Cabinet. Front, l. to r. Michael O'Kennedy, Desmond O'Malley, George Colley, Dr. Patrick Hillery, President of Ireland, Charles J. Haughey, Taoiseach of Ireland, Padraig Faulkner, Gerry Collins. Back, l. to r. Sylvester Barrett, Gene Fitzgerald, John Wilson, Ray McSharry, Maire Geoghegan Quinn, Dr. Michael Woods, Paddy Power, Tony Hedderman, Attorney General, Albert Reynolds.

him culminating in the disgraceful attempts to remove him from the leadership of Fianna Fail and from the Office of Taoiseach. It is said that, what does not destroy you only makes you stronger. This is the case with Charles Haughey. He has been severely tested and not found wanting. His fighting spirit is undiminished. He is now a strong and able leader of Fianna Fail. There is no one to equal him among the elected representatives to Dail Eireann. In a vigorous speech at the 1984 Fianna Fail Ard-Fheis he said:

"We are not going to be the generation of Fianna Fail who surrendered to the defeatist neo-colonial mentality. Fianna Fail will once again lead the Irish people out of the shadows of depression in a great national advance out into the sunlight of national pride and self-esteem, progress and achievement". . .

One of the surest traits of a great leader is his ability to learn from previous mistakes. Charles Haughey has that ability.

In December 1980, the Taoiseach, Charles Haughey met the British Prime Minister Margaret Thatcher. In spite of every effort on his part, Mrs. Thatcher would not yield on the official British attitude to North-East Ireland. She also appeared unwilling to make any effort to solve the British legacy of problems in that sector. The standard British answer was to send in more soldiers. The six North-Eastern counties of Ireland could be described as a training ground for British soldiers. It is here that they learn various methods of controlling riots, patrolling streets, covert actions and practical training in a wide variety of lethal weapons. Rubber and plastic bullets have been well tested against the citizens of Ireland who happen to live in the North-East sector. The experience will be useful when it comes to the point where they may have to control their own multi-blooded citizens on the British mainland. The citizens of North-East Ireland deserve better.

The deployment of underwater listening devices off the North-West coast of Ireland greatly aids the British and Americans in the detection of Soviet underwater traffic to and from their northern ports via the Norwegian Sea. Sophisticated radar devices, satellite link-ups and the readiness with which nuclear devices can be deployed in North-East Ireland is more than frightening for the average citizen. After the horrors of World War II, Ireland can certainly do without becoming the arena or tactical outpost on which a short but vicious Third World War will be fought. Again history has shown that in the majority of cases, reasonable political discussion with Britain has produced no results. Charles Haughey was correct in trying to reason with Margaret Thatcher. He is now aware, as are a large part of the population of Ireland, that reason does not get very far with her.

1981 was a general election year. The campaign commenced to a background of hunger strikes to the death, of a number of imprisoned Irishmen. The prisoners, known by the Irish term, "Republicans" or "I.R.A." and by the English term, "Terrorists", were incarcerated in a large fortified enclosure in North-East Ireland. They came to be known as the "H Block" prisoners as each block of cells looked like a giant H from the air. Many prisoners stood as candidates in the 1981 election. They captured a considerable percentage of Fianna Fail votes in the counties bordering the artificial frontier between South and North-East Ireland. The result was, Fianna Fail 78, Fine Gael 65 and Labour 15. Sinn Fein the Workers Party renamed themselves The Workers Party and achieved representation in the Dail for the first time. A new Coalition Government took office under Taoiseach Garret Fitzgerald. During the election campaign, the Coalition had pledged to move towards a reduction of the standard rate of tax.

On 27 January 1982, the Coalition Government collapsed on its first budget. The Government under Garret Fitzgerald proposed to extend the value added tax (V.A.T.) to children's shoes. This niggardly thinking on the part of Taoiseach Fitzgerald brought down his own government. Only Noel Browne voted with the coalition. During the election campaign, Fitzgerald did a U turn and announced that clothes and shoes for children under 10 would be exempt from tax.

A television debate was arranged between Garret Fitzgerald and Charles Haughey. Fitzgerald and his supporters were confident of winning. Advance publicity had built the debate to a high pitch. A huge percentage of the population watched or listened. It was here that Charles J. Haughey showed himself to be a true professional. Impeccably dressed, facing the camera and speaking clearly and concisely, he cut an impressive figure. During the debate Garret

Fitzgerald quoted interminable figures, shuffled papers, spoke rapidly and on several occasions managed to "lose" the majority of viewers. Polling day was on 18 February, 1982 and the forecasts were that Fianna Fail would secure about the same number of seats as all other parties and independents together. As counting of votes proceeded on the 19 February, it soon became clear that nobody would have an overall majority. The final results were: Fianna Fail 81; Fine Gael 63; Labour 15; Workers Party 3; Independents 4. The Independents were, John O'Connell, Neil Blaney, Tony Gregory and Jim Kemmy.

Garret Fitzgerald refused to concede defeat and Charles Haughey expressed his confidence that Fianna Fail would form the next government. C.J. was to be proven correct once again. The independent T.D., Dr. John O'Connell, would support Fianna Fail. An admirer of the ability of Charles Haughey, O'Connell was soon destined to join the ranks of Fianna Fail. The independent Donegal T.D., Neil Blaney, would support Fianna Fail. He wanted Charles Haughey to encourage employment by the promotion of the construction industry and he wanted a tougher public stance on the situation in the North of Ireland. For readers who are unfamiliar with the problem, the North-Eastern portion of the island of Ireland is forcibly held and governed by a foreign country, England. The counties under occupation are Derry, Antrim, Down, Armagh, Tyrone and Fermanagh. The six counties comprise a sizeable area of Ireland which has in total 32 counties. Many of our European partners seem to be unaware of the anomaly. French national newspapers, notably "Le Figaro" continue to place Dublin and Cork under the heading "Les Isles Britanniques", (The British Isles) in their weather forecast column. The independent T.D., Tony Gregory, had never supported any major party on a continuous basis and he was not a well known political figure. Gregory suddenly discovered that his vote would actually decide which party would form the next government. He immediately drew up a plan for inner city improvements in Dublin. This plan formed the basis for his negotiations with Charles Haughey and Garret Fitzgerald. When initial negotiations were completed, Gregory realised that Charles Haughey was the only leader with a serious grasp of the realities and difficulties facing Dublin's inner city. Gregory further realised that only C.J. had the ability and the strength of character to reliably carry out the agreed improvements' plan for the inner city. Charles Haughey's hard work and natural flair for getting things done coupled with an all round above average ability and intelligence saw a satisfactory conclusion to the Agreement. The Agreement was observed strictly until Fianna Fail left office at the general election of 24 November 1982. Jim Kemmy, the independent T.D. from Limerick, would vote with the Coalition parties. There were many areas of agreement betwen Fianna Fail and the Workers Party, but the Workers Party wanted to keep an independent stance. They were an up and coming party who hoped to eventually capture the Labour vote.

March 9th, 1982 was decision day for the Independents and the Workers Party. The Dail was crowded with relatives and friends of T.Ds. and a full quota of people from the press. Excitement was running high as everybody waited anxiously for the election of the new Taoiseach. The election of the Ceann Comhairle was first. Neil Blaney immediately proposed the Independent T.D. Dr. John O'Connell. He was returned to the Chair unopposed. It was then to the most important business of the day, the election of a new Taoiseach. Brian Lenihan proposed Charles Haughey. He was seconded by Ray McSharry from Sligo. The leader of the Labour Party, Michael O'Leary, proposed Garret Fitzgerald. He was seconded by Peter Barry. Joe Sherlock from the Workers Party proposed nobody but he stated that the Workers Party supported Charles Haughey for Taoiseach. Neil Blaney and Tony Gregory both stated that they supported C.J. Jim Kemmy, the Independent T.D. from Limerick then stated that he supported Garret Fitzgerald. There were demands for a roll call and John O'Connell, the Ceann Comhairle ordered the division bells to be rung. To the delight of journalists, an amusing incident then took place. The three Workers Party T.Ds. left the Chamber to talk and to attend to the calls of nature. They didn't seem to realise or else they forgot that the doors to the Chamber would be locked after three minutes. They found themselves locked out for the most crucial vote of the day. Joe Sherlock, the most experienced of the three, made a mad dash for the press gallery closely followed by his two colleagues. Then by a series of descending jumps, they found themselves in the

With U.S. President Ronald Reagan, March 1982.*(Photo: Courtesy deKun Photo.)*

Chamber to the astonishment of all present. Since that episode, all entrances to the Chamber are locked for divisions.

The voting was 79 for Fitzgerald, 86 for Haughey. Charles J. Haughey was soon on his way to the President to be formally appointed Taoiseach for the second time. He left Aras an Uachtarain in a determined and confident mood. He was once more the confirmed leader of Fianna Fail and now Taoiseach. He reflected on the recent past when petty squabbles and jealousies threatened both himself and the party. That was now in the past. It was time to look to the future and choose a Cabinet which would work well together. There was no point in tolerating ministers who would continue to plot his downfall. Real and strong leadership was necessary and he would not shirk the challenge. In the 1979-'81 Fianna Fail government, it was clear that Colley had exerted too much influence. To the extent that the power of the leader was curtailed and the power of decision was limited. The end result was that the leader appeared weak.

Colley was again looking for the position of Tanaiste or deputy prime minister. He would accept no other ministerial post. He was

Charles and Maureen Haughey with U.S. First Lady, Nancy Reagan.
(Photo: Courtesy deKun Photo.)

left out altogether. A new and more decisive Charles Haughey was leader. C.J. was however generous enough to give Des O'Malley Trade, Commerce and Tourism and Martin O'Donoghue got Education. Charles Haughey was always willing to put the common good ahead of petty party political squabbles. Not everyone thought likewise. Grudges were held against him and it was sad to see people who could have offered much to this country, lose sight of what they were elected to do and instead submit to their own personal whims and petty jealousies.

About six weeks before the February 1982 election a young politically immature T.D. called Charles McCreevy gave an interview to the Tribune, a Sunday newspaper. In the interview McCreevy criticised the direction of the Fianna Fail party. This was a veiled public attack on the leader of the party. McCreevy, though relatively inexperienced, was a most vociferous young man who clearly enjoyed his new found media fame. Everybody clamoured for his opinion on anything and everything. He gave it freely. Charles Haughey decided to call for his expulsion from the party. McCreevy resigned. Just about a week later the February 1982 general election was called and McCreevy was back with Fianna Fail. His media fame did him little harm and he was elected easily.

The post election period was a busy one for Charles Haughey. Along with negotiations with Blaney, Gregory and the Workers Party, he had to prepare to defend his position as leader against some members of the Fianna Fail party. Although he tried very hard to reason with his opponents, it was all to no avail. Some were hell bent on getting their own way no matter what the cost to the party. The Sunday Tribune predicted that an assault on the leadership of Charles Haughey would take place. Desmond O'Malley was happy to state that he would be a challenger for the Party's nomination for Taoiseach when the Fianna Fail Parliamentary Party met at Leinster House. The Irish Independent published the names of over half of the Fianna Fail T.Ds whom they alleged were supporters of O'Malley for the leadership. Many were embarrassed by the unwanted publicity. The crucial parliamentary meeting was scheduled for the Thursday after the election. Shortly after the commencement of the debate, Desmond O'Malley stood up and declared that he was withdrawing his name and his challenge for the leadership. Charles J. Haughey was then unanimously declared leader of Fianna Fail and was chosen as the Party's nominee for Taoiseach. The Parliamentary Party meeting over, he made no petty or vindictive statements. He got on with the job in hand . . . the formation of a government.

Shortly after becoming Taoiseach, Charles Haughey made an offer to Dick Burke that generated immense public interest and many column inches of print. He offered the post of E.E.C. Commissioner to Burke, a Fine Gael T.D. Burke was an experienced man in Europe. He liked his job and he got on extremely well in Brussels. Many of his Fine Gael colleagues insisted that he should not accept the post of E.E.C. Commissioner. Yet he was clearly the most experienced man for the job. By Friday, 26 March 1982, Burke had made up his mind that he would take the job. It was clear that he would continue to perform well, but the violently vociferous reaction of his Fine Gael colleagues was incomprehensible to the normal thinking voter. In the ensuing by

35

An Taoiseach Charles J. Haughey with Senator Edward Kennedy.
(Photo: Courtesy deKun Photo.)

election in Dublin West, Burke's constituency, Liam Skelly won the seat for Fine Gael. Skelly has since gained the attention of the media for some of his speeches on our excellent police and teaching profession.

The month of May 1982 saw the outbreak of what was to be a short but vicious war between Britain and Argentina. Argentina had been negotiating with Britain over the return of the Malvinas or Falkland Islands in the South Atlantic for endless years. The Argentinians decided to occupy the islands. Britain went to war with what appeared to be a fearsome array of weaponry. Ireland and Italy stayed neutral. France had already sold some exocet missiles to Argentina and a real war would test their effectiveness. In the first week of May 1982, the aged Argentine Cruiser, the General Belgrano steamed home on the high seas and in neutral waters. Without warning, the Belgrano was hit by torpedoes from the nuclear powered British submarine, the Conqueror. The official story from London was that the ancient warship was about to attack the British naval task force and anyhow it posed a considerable threat to the same force. Three hundred and sixty eight young sailors never saw their homeland again. Charles Haughey, Taoiseach of Ireland, publicly regretted and condemned the sinking of the Belgrano. A torrent of criticism and adverse comment flowed in his direction. The Taoiseach's prediction was vindicated later when it was subsequently proved that the Belgrano was in fact in international waters and steaming away from the Malvinas.

Trade sanctions were imposed against Argentina for landing troops on the disputed islands. Ireland and Italy refused to renew the sanctions. The British press screamed invective against Ireland and in particular against the Taoiseach Charles Haughey. Shortly after, the British warship the Sheffield was sunk by an exocet missile supplied to the Argentine air force by the French. There were protests from the British but no particular invective against the French president. The French were excited. Their exocet missiles

An Taoiseach Charles J. Haughey with the West German Chancellor Helmut Schmidt in Bonn, July 1982.

had turned in a star performance. It took only one direct hit from one exocet to sink the modern warship the Sheffield. Enquiries and orders for the missile poured in from all over the world. Nobody protested too much about such trafficking in sophisticated, vicious and deadly weapons.

Later Tam Dalyell M.P. sought the truth about the whole sordid affair. He was muzzled at every turn in his investigation. When it looked as if he might cause major embarrassment to Mrs. Thatcher, the submarine's log book went mysteriously missing. End of investigation. How many returned to Charles Haughey and congratulated him on his justified stance in the whole sordid affair. Instead, he was accused of destroying Anglo-Irish relations.

One man, Charles Haughey Taoiseach of Ireland, stood up and behaved as the leader of an independent state. In spite of all the criticisms and the contrived animosities directed towards him, Charles Haughey continued to act as a fearless leader of an independent country. He did exactly what he was democratically elected to do.

The Malvinas/Falklands war demonstrated once again the fragility of peace in the world. We now live in a world so crowded with fearsome nuclear weapons that it is possible for mankind to utterly destroy itself in an extremely short space of time. It is on the question of Disarmament that Charles Haughey has proved himself to be a statesman of international standing. His speech to the United Nations General Assembly on 11 July 1982 is reckoned to be his finest delivery to date.

Mr. President,

It is just four years since world leaders met previously in this hall for the First Special Session on Disarmament. Hopes were high; world public attention was engaged, speeches were made; proposals were outlined; and an important document on disarmament emerged.

What has happened since? In that four years world expenditure on armaments has increased by over $200 billion. The number of nuclear warheads has increased to some 40,000. And the hands of the clock of the Bulletin of Atomic Scientists which monitors the dangers of nuclear war have moved appreciably closer to midnight.

Some favourite leisure moments.   *(Photo: Courtesy The Sunday Times.)*

Now we meet again for the Second Special Session. For the next few weeks public attention will focus on this hall. Speaker after speaker will come to this rostrum to advocate disarmament. Concerned about a rising tide of popular concern in each of our countries, we will each speak movingly of the waste of resources and the growing dangers arising from world armaments.

When it ends, this Special Session too will have produced a document—a comprehensive programme for disarmament. It may be the result of many difficult compromises. But it will no doubt be a worthy document—one fit to take its place as the latest in a sequence of other worthy documents and pacts beginning with the Hague Conference of 1899—all of them directed to reducing armaments and outlawing war.

But will anything change in the real world? Will there be one less nuclear weapon, one less missile, one less tank, or rocket or gun? Will the wealthy and powerful countries and the major alliances take any real or serious step to halt, if not to reverse, the arms race between them? Will Third World countries show any less willingness to divert their resources towards a build-up of armaments for prestige reasons or because of regional rivalries? Will any of us begin to act as we speak? Will we conform our policies to our rhetoric?

The record so far is a melancholy one. Throughout this century there have been countless disarmament conferences, disarmament committees, disarmament commissions and disarmament negotiations. Various pacts and treaties have been signed. But this century has seen the two greatest wars in human history; and today we are poised for a third, which if it ever happens, promises to be the last.

It is perhaps paradoxical, but the capacity of ordinary men and women to understand the situation in which the world now finds itself has been numbed by repetition. Conferences, speeches, articles, books, television, describe our situation but it does not really sink in.

To make the facts sink home one would almost have to imagine what a visitor from elsewhere would report on our planet if he studied our present condition.

He would report first that the dominant species on this planet seems to have an innate capacity for war.

He would describe the political organisation of the planet—divided as it is into some 160 sovereign states. Some are large and powerful, some are small and weak. They group themselves in various ways—East, West, North, South—but each claims to be sovereign as against all the others. He would note that these sovereign states, either individually or in groups, have a tendency to frequent conflict; and that in consequence they tend to distrust each other and to believe that their security can only be assured if they constantly prepare themselves for possible conflict.

He would have to report however on a strange paradox. The preparation for conflict which no one wants, increases mistrust and makes it more likely that conflict will occur. Every nation preparing for possible conflict is convinced that it is thereby adding to its security. But the overall effect of these efforts by each to add to its own security is an immense increase in the insecurity of all.

Our imaginary traveller would report a second great puzzle about our world. Human need is great and resources and wealth are very unevenly distributed. But our planet can nevertheless devote a very great part of these resources to weapons of destruction.

But there should be no need to imagine such an outside observer to understand fully our present situation. The stark facts are available in many recent reports. Let me cite three such points which describe clearly the peril of our situation.

- Total world expenditure on armaments is now over 600 billion dollars. This is the highest total in human history.
- The nuclear weapons now available and poised for use have an explosive power more than one million times that of the bomb which destroyed Hiroshima killing 150,000 people in 1945. I repeat—today there could be one million Hiroshimas.
- The two major nuclear powers between them probably now have more than 15,000 strategic nuclear warheads. This is three times what they had 12 years ago in 1970.

It can only be because our senses have been numbed by repetition that humanity has come to accept these chilling facts as a normal part of life on our planet today. The irony is that we describe as "realists" those who study and plan and produce theories relating to the development and use of these weapons. Those who would reject

41

this reality and seek to change it or who regard it as monstrous and unacceptable are, strangely enough, called "idealists".

How is it that humanity has come to accept this? Why is there such a discrepancy—one might better call it a gulf—between what political leaders, and I include all of us, say on disarmament on occasions such as this and what we do in the real world about armaments?

The easy answer is for each of us somehow to distance ourselves from the steady growth in armaments—to speak of the "arms race" as if it were an evil force which existed in its own right. In this way each of us can conveniently speak of an evil process, detached from ourselves, which endangers the world. But the reality is that it is not some separate process or evil force which has led us to where we are but rather the sum total of the measures taken by each of 160 sovereign states to protect its own security. The consequence is the most fearful insecurity for all.

But even if we see that the steady build up in armaments is not an impersonal force but the sum of a series of separate human decisions by nations in search of security, we still want to lay the blame elsewhere—on the "other" side. East blames West and West blames East. Small countries speak of the super-powers, poor countries of the industrialised world. Industrialised countries in turn point to regional rivalries and the arms build-up in less developed countries where many of the wars of recent decades have taken place.

It is precisely this kind of thinking which has brought us to where we are. Every country thinks its own subjective intentions are good but it believes it has good reason to mistrust the intentions of others.

Unless we recognise this paradox and try to deal with it our rhetoric will remain forever divorced from reality. Every country will continue to display its good intentions in speeches made here about disarmament. But because of its suspicions of the intentions of potential opponents, each country will continue to act differently in the real world in order to build up its own security.

Even then, as it builds up armaments, each country continues to believe in its own good intentions; and each fails to see why its potential rivals should be suspicious. But there is often a great gap between a nation's view of its own intentions and the way in which those intentions are perceived by potential opponents. It is there that the human dilemma—the dilemma of disarmament really lies.

I believe that the greatest need at present is to recognise this dilemma and to try to find ways to deal with it. Otherwise our speeches and our good intentions about disarmament will forever remain divorced from reality.

Let me emphasise this point. We have been brought to where we are, not because of some abstract or evil force but because of inherent feelings of mistrust, fear and insecurity between nations in a world of sovereign states. Mistrust leads to a build-up of armaments. A build up of arms in turn increases mistrust. The result is a spiral where the direction is always upward. Step by step the process acquires a dynamic of its own.

The build up of arms and the growth of mistrust between nations are mutually reinforcing. From this, I believe, two important consequences follow:

> First, both aspects of the problem must be tackled in parallel.
>
> On the one hand, we need serious and sustained efforts to negotiate disarmament. On the other hand, we need a corresponding effort to build and strengthen international institutions through which the rule of law among nations can be promoted and developed and insecurity and mistrust decreased.
>
> Second, if each step taken to build up armaments increases mistrust, then it follows that each step, however small, to reduce armaments could help to ease distrust. In other words if the direction of the spiral could once be reversed, the same dynamic interaction between the level of armaments and the level of trust among nations would still apply. Then each step—even a small step showing restraint by one side could evoke a corresponding step towards restraint on the other.

But these are general points. How do we apply them in practice? In particular how can we use this second special session of the United Nations General Assembly and the immense interest it has generated in public opinion around the world to begin at last to take actual steps towards disarmament?

I would suggest that:

> First, we must use the occasion of such a major conference and such public interest to confirm in the broadest way the general commitment of the nations of the world to the concept of disarmament. This should naturally include the ideal of General and Complete Disarmament already endorsed by the General Assembly over 20 years ago. However distant that ideal might now seem it must be retained as the ultimate goal of disarmament efforts.

> Second, we need a Comprehensive Programme for Disarmament as the outcome of this Assembly Session. Such a programme would give coherence to the various disarmament discussions and negotiations now under way in different fora; and set realistic goals for those discussions.

> Third, a general goal and a programme for working towards it are not enough. We badly need some first steps. If the Programme is not to remain something on paper only like so many proposals and agreements in the past, then some practical first steps must now be taken to give it life and impetus.

As to the first of these points—the goal of general and complete disarmament—no doubt this aspiration will be reflected suitably as the ultimate goal in the document adopted at the end of this session. On the second point—the comprehensive programme for disarmament—considerable work has already been done and the next month of discussions in this Assembly will, I hope, bring that programme to fruition.

What I would like to do here, however, is to concentrate on the third point—that is the series of steps which I believe need now to be taken in order to give credibility to the programme and offer hope to the world. These steps should be taken by each country according to its capacity and its role in the growth of the armaments which have so endangered our planet.

This means above all, the nuclear weapons states, whose build-up of nuclear armaments is most dangerous.

44

I would offer a list of points on which I believe the nuclear powers should be ready to act:

- First; they need to recognise and accept that, as one important recent article put it:
  "the one clearly definable fire-break against the world wide disaster of general nuclear war is the one that stands between all other kinds of conflict and any use whatsoever of nuclear weapons. To keep that fire-break wide and strong is in the deepest interests of all mankind."
  I believe that the nuclear powers need to consider seriously what methods or agreements they might work out providing against the first use by any of them of nuclear weapons.

- Second; I believe that the nuclear powers should take account of the many public calls for a freeze on nuclear weapons at least to the extent of agreeing on such a freeze or moratorium for, say, an initial two year period. This would mean agreeing not to add to the existing number of warheads or of delivery vehicles for nuclear weapons on either side over a two-year trial period when serious negotiations such as the so-called START talks are underway. Of course if this two-year moratorium should increase trust on either side it could be extended year by year while real and substantive disarmament measures are being worked out.

- Third; The world absolutely needs a comprehensive test ban treaty. The Partial Test Ban Treaty of 1963 which banned explosions in the atmosphere and was signed by three of the nuclear powers is clearly insufficient. In the period since the Treaty was signed in 1963 some 800 nuclear tests have taken place. This is significantly more than the total of 500 tests which had occurred in the whole period from 1945 to 1963.

- Fourth; The SALT II Agreement which both sides now abide by should be ratified. If they can abide by the Treaty in practice as they seem to be doing, why should they not ratify the Treaty and thus increase confidence somewhat on both sides?

- Fifth; We welcome the efforts to get the so-called START talks underway. We hope that all of the nuclear powers can eventually be brought to participate in such talks; and that the proposals made will be serious and well intentioned and not merely designed to win over public opinion around the world.

These are five basic steps which, I believe, the nuclear powers need to take and take urgently. But just as the build-up of armaments extends beyond the nuclear powers so too the steps which need now to be taken must cover more than nuclear weapons.

There is an urgent need in particular to address the insidious problem of other weapons of mass destruction. As long ago as 1925, the use of poisonous gas was banned by international agreement. Furthermore, bacteriological weapons which are designed deliberately to spread the very diseases which mankind has struggled for centuries to defeat or control have more recently been prohibited. Nonetheless, the threat of chemical weapons still remains. There are still huge stockpiles of nerve gas in existence and no effective agreement has yet been reached on destroying them. In fact, the major powers still appear to be actively engaged in research and development on these weapons.

Other weapons of mass destruction are contemplated or being developed—for example, radiological weapons which pervert the life-saving discovery of X-Rays to destructive ends. In addition, concern is mounting in recent years that weapons for use in outer space may be developed. These weapons are already on the drawing board and money is being spent on research. If we wait until the weapons actually appear, then experience shows there is very little possibility that they will be negotiated away.

In the field of conventional weapons, I believe the greatest need is to work out methods for calculation of military budgets and expenditure on armaments on a common, universally accepted basis. If this could be done, the next stage would be to work out agreements to reduce those budgets on all sides and on a graduated basis.

These are all important first steps in the area of arms control and disarmament. Each is practicable and given the necessary will it should be possible by carrying them through in practice to give the spiral that vital downward turn.

But what of the other side of the question—the distrust and tensions among nations which stimulate and are in turn reinforced by the arms race?

It is vital to address this through efforts to strengthen international security which should both complement and reinforce disarmament measures. This is surely evident at present. As this Assembly meets here to discuss disarmament we are all uneasily aware that four wars at least are raging in the world at present. None of those wars at the moment I speak, shows much sign of being easily checked.

Wars may once have been the only method of settling disputes among nations. But as Pope John Paul II said recently, expressing the hopes of hundreds of millions the world over, "Today, the scale and the horror of modern warfare, whether nuclear or not, make it totally unacceptable as a means of settling differences between nations".—in particular the United Nations and its institutions and procedures which should have made war obsolete. These institutions badly need to be strengthened and made effective. And the nations of the world must learn to use those instruments and procedures rather than seeking to vindicate their rights by resort to war.

An important step to show confidence in these institutions could be taken, I believe, if the five nuclear powers—who as it happens are also the permanent members of the Security Council—would use the Security Council and its procedures to give binding security guarantees to the non-nuclear states which would ensure that no nuclear power will ever use nuclear weapons against a non-nuclear power. This would give an important fillup to the Nuclear Non-Proliferation Treaty—that essential dyke against the spread of nuclear weapons.

But more than any single step of this kind it is important, in my view, that the nations of the world make use of this Organisation—the United Nations—which is almost universal in its membership. It provides procedures and a code of conduct to govern relations between nations which, if properly used, can play an important part in easing mistrust and creating a respect for law between states.

This will mean restraint and respect for these procedures by all states. It will mean too that States must constantly make a deliberate choice—to use the instrumentality of the United Nations and its institutions to the full—rather than resorting only to their own strength to vindicate the principles which they rightly want to uphold.

We live in a time when, for better or worse, the human species on this planet has entered a new era. We know now the limits of our planet and its resources. We are a single human community to an increasing extent in our global travel and global communications. But what is most significant—and frightening—is that at this stage in its long history, humanity in our day has at last uncovered the fearful power through which it can destroy itself and extinguish much of the other life on the planet. As Arthur Koestler has said, "man has always had to live with the prospect of his death as an individual, but today, mankind has to live with the prospect of its own extinction."

At just this moment in human history, however, humanity has also created and—however falteringly—an Assembly in which virtually every nation on earth is represented; an admirable code of conduct for relations between nations and a family of international institutions grouped around the United Nations which provide many useful procedures and provisions for settling disputes and promoting cooperation between them.

In other words at the moment of our greatest peril in all of human history when distrust and suspicion between nations and peoples has led to a massive build-up of armaments which now threaten our very existence, we have at hand—however weak and ineffectual it may seem at times—the very instrument we need to establish and maintain the rule of law and assure the security of nations, large and small. It is vital that we use it.

It has been said that wars begin in men's minds. Long before the first shot is fired, fear and distrust have prepared the battleground.

The word "peace" has no meaning and no value if it is only to be a time in which we prepare for further wars. The peace we enjoy now is fragmented and vulnerable and could so easily be lost. As none of us could escape the consequences of another general war, none of us should try to evade our responsibility. Public opinion around the world is mobilised; the Palme Commission report will be helpful and useful. The launching of a World Disarmament Campaign is also welcome and can support these efforts. It is now for those who carry

48

the responsibility for national decisions to face those responsibilities.

Every country, whatever its size or importance, must do what it can to help ward off the catastrophe threatening all humanity. Those who are militarily powerful have the primary responsibility to disarm. Others—countries like my own who are not directly involved in the arms race—have the responsibility to do all in their power to help resolve conflict, to relieve tension and to build up an irresistible strength of world public opinion against the use of force in international affairs and to do everything we can to remove war from men's minds.

It is my earnest hope, therefore, that this Special Session of the General Assembly on Disarmament which is being attended by so many world leaders and which has evoked such hope around the world will, indeed, be a new beginning.

- We need a new commitment to the long-term goal of general disarmament,
- We need a coherent and comprehensive programme through which we may hope to get there,
- We need some important first steps in practice to give substance and reality to that programme,
- And we need a new commitment to use the United Nations and its family of institutions to the full and to strengthen them and make them more effective so that nations may begin to find justice and security which they seek—not in a wasteful, futile and dangerous build-up of armaments but in the increasing application of the rule of law among nations.

Thank you, Mr. President.

*   *   *

In August 1982, the Taoiseach Charles Haughey was on holidays on the tiny island of Inismhicileáin situated off the Kerry coast. John Connolly, the Attorney General, occupied an exclusive apartment in the exclusive Pilot View scheme overlooking Dublin bay from Dalkey. An acquaintance called Malcolm McArthur paid him a visit. McArthur asked to stay for a few days and Connolly,

Charles Haughey with his brother, Father Eoghan and his sister Maureen.

suspecting nothing, readily agreed to his request. Connolly's generosity was to precipitate a crisis for both himself and the Taoiseach. McArthur was arrested at Connolly's apartment and charged with a variety of crimes which included the murder of a young nurse called Bridie Gargan. John Connolly although completely innocent of any complicity in the affair, had to resign as Attorney General and the Taoiseach Charles Haughey had to weather the subsequent storm of innuendo and criticism. McArthur was sent for trial to the Central Criminal Court. He pleaded guilty to the murder of Nurse Gargan and he was sentenced to penal servitude for life. The actual hearing lasted less than ten minutes. There was a further media outcry of cover-up etc. However, most people seemed to have overlooked the fact that it is normal legal practice not to call witnesses when the accused pleads guilty to the crime. The mandatory sentence is simply handed down in accordance with the law. The year 1982 was to continue to be an eventful one in the life of Taoiseach Charles Haughey.

The 1977 general election brought a young Kildare man to the Dail for the first time. His name was Charles McCreevy. Less than five years later he was plotting the downfall of the democratically elected leader of Fianna Fail. The fact that the leader of Fianna Fail happened to be Taoiseach of Ireland did not seem to matter to McCreevy. The fact that the majority of the Irish electorate wanted the country to be led by Charles Haughey at that particular point in time, did not seem to be of any importance to McCreevy. The challenge was given maximum prior publicity. O'Malley and O'Donoghue resigned from the Cabinet in order to boost the challenge to the leadership. They were thinking of themselves in terms of Taoisigh as well of course. By this abdication of the will of the electorate, they hoped to bring down the Taoiseach of the day, Charles Haughey. It was unprecedented in the history of any political party in Ireland that the elected members would challenge the leadership of the party while in government.

In a tough speech on R.T.E., Charles Haughey stated that the dissidents were a small minority within Fianna Fail. "They would have to stand up and be counted", he said. He was going to insist on a roll call and demand the total support of his Cabinet. He was their democratically elected leader and he was entitled to the support of all party members, he added.

On Wednesday 6 October, 1982, a motion of no confidence in the leadership of Charles Haughey was tabled by McCreevy. On a roll call the motion was defeated by 58 votes to 22.

October 1982 was a busy month for Charles Haughey. The Fianna Fail T.D., Bill Loughnane died. That left the government down one crucial vote. In the same month Fianna Fail launched their manifesto, "The Way Forward". Jim Gibbons T.D. for Fianna Fail had two heart attacks which left him unable to attend Dail voting. During this time the Fianna Fail government was constantly in danger of defeat. On some divisions, the government was saved only by the Ceann Comhairle's casting vote. The crunch came on 24 November 1982. The government was defeated on its economic plan by 82 votes to 80. The short life of the Fianna Fail government led by Charles Haughey had been an action-packed one. The galloping inflation had been reduced by 8 points to 13%. The government had compiled an economic plan that was widely acclaimed. The Fianna

Standing at the front door of Abbeville.   *(Photo: Fionan O'Connell.)*

Fail proposal for a referendum on abortion was widely approved. The government and Charles Haughey vigorously defended Irish neutrality and spoke out fearlessly on matters of international importance.

The November election campaign became quite dramatic when Garret Fitzgerald stated that he hoped to have implemented the machinery to cover an all-Ireland judiciary and police force. It was an error of judgment on his part and it served to diminish his credibility amcng the voting public. The average Irish citizen was understandably not too keen on having the Royal Ulster Constabulary exercising a measure of control in the Republic of Ireland. In fact the Attorney General, John Murray was so shocked at the suggestions of Fitzgerald that he felt it necessary to issue a public statement to the effect that such policing proposals would undermine the effectiveness and independence of the forces of law and order and the sovereign institutions of the State.

Charles Haughey put on his usual brilliant performance for the television debate between Fitzgerald and himself. He lost the election. Results were Fianna Fail 75, Fine Gael 70, Labour 16, Workers Party 2, Independents 3.

CHAPTER 4

THE LEADER

On 2 November 1982, Fianna Fail produced the wording for the Referendum on Abortion. It was proposed to insert an article banning abortion into the Constitution of the Republic of Ireland. Much debate had taken place on the question of abortion in Ireland.

In November 1982 Fianna Fail published an acceptable wording for the Referendum on the Eight Amendment of the Constitution. After the November 1982 General Election the Coalition Government of Fine Gael and Labour returned to power. They decided that they could improve on the Fianna Fail wording and they attempted a new wording of their own. The wording was unclear and unacceptable to most people.

In an effort to dispel the fudged approach of the new Coalition Government on the issue of abortion in Ireland, Charles Haughey re-stated the case for the general acceptance of the original Fianna Fail wording. On 20 April 1983, he delivered a major speech on the Pro-Life Amendment Bill. He said:

"Fianna Fail reaffirms its full support for the wording of the Pro-Life Amendment in the Bill as published by the Fianna Fail Government in November 1982.

It is by far the best wording that has been produced and should now be put to the people. It won a broad consensus of support at the time it was published and it still retains that widespread support today.

In the drafting of the Amendment, which was given prolonged and most careful consideration by the Fianna Fail Government and by the two Attorney Generals who advised it, the views and advice of representatives of all the principal Churches were sought and taken into account. Great care was taken to ensure that the proposed wording would not be sectarian or seen to be sectarian, but would reflect to the greatest possible extent the broad consensus that exists within the community on the subject of abortion. In this regard we would draw attention to the official comment from the Standing Committee of the General Synod of the Church of Ireland on 16th November, 1982, which, while reiterating certain reservations made prior to the publication of the wording stated:

'Having now studied the text of the proposed 8th Amendment to the constitution the standing Committee makes the following observations:

1. We recognise that an attempt has been made to take account of the complexity of this subject and the views expressed by our own and other Churches.
2. In particular we are relieved that the proposed wording of the Amendment acknowledges the right to life of the unborn with due regard to the equal right to life of the mother'.

On the basis of the degree of consensus achieved, both major Parties sought and received support from the electorate in November, 1982, on the understanding that they would introduce the Amendment as soon as possible, and in the case of Fine Gael, before 31st March, 1983.

Fianna Fail was not the first Party to give a commitment to introduce a Pro-Life Amendment. Since giving its word, however, it has maintained an absolutely principled and consistent approach to the issue. The demand for such an Amendment has to be seen as a reasonable one, which we believe enjoys wide support among the Irish people. To the extent that some people and groups have misgivings either about the wording or the principle of the Amendment, their concerns can be put before the people in the course of the referendum campaign, and be duly decided upon by them. After solemn commitments have been made by the principal parties during three successive General Elections, it would be a gross breach of public faith to delay any further putting this issue before the people. The Constitution indeed states that, 'the people have the right in final appeal, to decide all questions of national policy, according to the requirements of the common good'.

It is no derogation of the functions either of the Supreme Court or of the Oireachtas that, on a question of human rights, the basic principle that is to guide the future actions of both should be a matter for decision by the people.

Fianna Fail does not regard the proposed new wording put forward by the Fine Gael Leader as fulfilling that Party's solemn promises and commitments, nor does it provide any effective guarantees against the introduction of abortion into Ireland. It is not a genuine Pro-Life Amendment, and moreover, it directly contradicts the positive approach specifically recommended by the Fine Gael Leader in his Ard-Fheis speech in October, 1982 and in his comments on the published Bill in early November. Fianna Fail deplore the way in which the inconsistencies, contradictory statements, and reversals of policy of the Taoiseach, Dr. Fitzgerald have caused a great deal of unnecessary division and confusion, and created scope for misrepresentation both at home and abroad. By contrast Fianna Fail has from the beginning adopted a calm and responsible approach to this issue, endeavouring to keep the political debate reasoned and restrained and to ensure that public debate be largely conducted on non-party lines.

Fianna Fail rejects as of no significance the objections first put forward by the present Attorney General, which the Taoiseach has very late in the day fastened on to as an explanation for his abandonment of undertakings solemnly given and accepted in good faith. These objections have been clearly and specifically shown by expert legal and medical opinion to be without foundation. Fianna Fail is frankly appalled at some of the intemperate and emotive language recently employed by the Taoiseach, which seeks to arouse needless fears and anxieties and to replace calm and mature debate by political invective.

It is also in our view highly improper for the Taoiseach to maintain that the Supreme Court should interpret constitutional guarantees in such a way as to render them worthless.

Fianna Fail wish to see the parliamentary debates on this matter concluded as quickly as possible and the original pro-life amendment placed before the people. The Dail should come to its decision without any further delay. The Fine Gael Party should now end the confusion which it has caused among some members of the general public by reverting to its original position and supporting the present Bill and wording which let it be remembered their own Government introduced."

After much internal debate, confusion and soul searching, the Coalition Government accepted the original wording. Voting on the Eight Amendment took place in September 1983. From then on, the right to life of the unborn has been protected by the Constitution of the Republic of Ireland. Now Article 40.3.3. of the Constitution of Ireland states: "The State acknowledges the right to life of the unborn and, with due regard to the equal right to life of the mother, guarantees in its laws to respect, and, as far as practicable, by it laws to defend and vindicate that right."

*   *   *

On 27 January 1983, one of the national newspapers, the Irish Press, published a two page political profile of Charles Haughey. Was it meant to be a political obituary? If so, they overlooked the fact that a body is necessary to validate an obit. On that same day Ben Briscoe T.D. had an emotional realization. He made a suitably emotional speech at a Fianna Fail party meeting, the gist of same was, that in the interests of Fianna Fail Charles Haughey should resign. And in keeping with the best romantic traditions, Briscoe ended his speech with the words, "I love you Charlie Haughey". Quick as a flash Charlie replied, "And I love you too Ben". This humorous reply illustrated once again the clear and calm thinking of Charles Haughey under intense pressure. He has never cracked while under pressure and he has never become over emotional. His realisations and actions are controlled by intelligent judgement rather than by emotion. Charles Haughey is always at his calmest in times of stress. It is then that he displays the cool nerve and all of the qualities that have made him a great leader.

To those who opposed him, Charles Haughey spoke publicly. The following extracts are gleaned from a statement issued from the Fianna Fail Press Office and from an interview with Gerald Barry on the radio programme "This Week" relayed on the Sunday prior to the crucial vote. Charles Haughey said: "The Fianna Fail that I lead is not, and will not be, a Party of the right or the left. It is the Party of the nation with a special care for the old, the poor and those who are economically and socially disadvantaged. It must also be the Party of those countless young people who are now concerned about their future in our society.

"My conviction has always been that the people of Ireland must cherish and enhance their own way of life, their separate identity, their values and their culture. Fianna Fail's purpose must always be to uphold the cause of the unity of Ireland, her national independence, and her right to decide her place in the world and her role in international affairs . . .

"Many people now clearly identify, where the basic problem in the Party is. I was elected as leader of the Party by democratic majority, a small majority, and the people who were beaten at that time have never accepted that situation and have constituted themselves a group within the Party ever since, anxious to avail of any opportunity to exploit any position that arises to damage me as leader of the party. That's the basis of all the trouble. If these recent events hadn't happened there would be some other occasion when they would have mobilised to try and put me out of the leadership. That is their total motivation in political life. They're not concerned with the success of Fianna Fail. They're concerned primarily with their own position in Fianna Fail and to remove me from the leadership . . .

"I have said of course I must accept some blame for the present state of the Party, to what extent again I think only history will decide. All I can say about that is that I have tried, I have tried to the best of my ability. I have been patient with people. I have put up with a great deal, and as I said, I kept people in my Government and in positions of authority in the Party when every political instinct would have told me not to do so. In fact I am now blamed that I didn't put people out of the Party long ago, but I've tried as I say to preserve the unity of the Party, to try and keep it together as best I could, keep the diverse factions together. Now if I didn't succeed in that, then of course I must accept some of the blame, but I believe the blame lies primarily elsewhere, in those who from the word go, from the day I became leader, refused to accept that position and fought this battle ever since, which is now culminating . . .

"Politics is my life. I fight battles, I try and move things forward, do what I can, achieve progress, improvements, look after the old

In the peaceful grounds at Abbeville secluded from the hustle and bustle of politics. *(Photo: Fionan O'Connell.)*

people, look after the disadvantaged. I try to implement my political philosophy to the best I can, maybe if I didn't try and do any of these things then I wouldn't incur any hostility anywhere. If you don't try and do anything, then I don't think anybody bothers very much with you. But I am quite satisfied that I have conducted my political activities as I believe they should be conducted. I tried to do things, I particularly tried to keep the Party together and I'm quite satisfied that I have discharged my duty to the Party and to the people as satisfactory."

On 1 February 1983, the young Donegal T.D., Clem Coughlan was killed in a tragic motoring accident. The dreadful news was hardly absorbed by the public when certain voices within Fianna Fail were clamouring for a vote on the leadership. They called for a parliamentary meeting on Friday, 4 February 1983 to decide the issue. The haste was indecent. Clem Coughlan had only been buried the day before. Jim Tunney T.D., Chairman of the Fianna Fail Parliamentary Party displayed some human respect when he declared that he would not call a meeting over the dead body of a colleague in the Dail. So soon was Clem Coughlan forgotten and now the race was on to bury Charlie Haughey.

Ben Briscoe T.D. who was again in a mood for rather emotional and romantic utterings stated: "I am prepared to lie down and die politically for what I do. I am very proud of my party. I am certain they will make the right decision". They did. Charles Haughey retained the leadership of Fianna Fail by 40 votes to 33. A large crowd of supporters had kept vigil outside Leinster House while the debate was in progress. When the result was announced, the cheering and applause was loud, joyful and sustained. The third attempt to oust Charles Haughey as leader of Fianna Fail had failed dismally.

The 1983 Fianna Fail Ard-Fheis concluded a busy but extremely successful month for Charles Haughey. He was given a rapturous welcome by the delegates and supporters. He extended a warm welcome to all of the media people. He asked that there would be no confrontations and no recriminations. As far as he was concerned, the earlier divisions were in the past and were to be forgotten. The great task of building up the party for the next general election was to be initiated at this Ard-Fheis. His, was a brilliant speech of

61

reconciliation, of encouragement and of looking ahead to a better future. "The difficulties we have had are now behind us", he said. "We are again on the high road as a great unified party; there will be no turning back; we face the future eager and determined". Such is the measure of the man. He had worked hard for the party and he deserved better than what he had so recently received from those who were mandated by the people to support their democratically elected leader. In his mind however, there was no place for recrimination or for petty barbed remarks at those who had earlier opposed his leadership. He saw his role as leader clearly. It was his task to construct a powerful party destined to rule with compassion and justice. His presidential address created a buoyant mood for the future. It was without doubt Charlie Haughey's finest hour and a most memorable Ard-Fheis.

A rather historic political event occurred in June 1984. U.S. President Ronald Reagan visited Ireland. It was an election year in the U.S. and the 40 million Irish-American votes were important to him. During the tour he remained silent on the political situation in North-East Ireland except for some references condemning violence in that sector. One of the most bizarre happenings of that visit concerned the attempts of Garret Fitzgerald and his government to deprive Charles Haughey, Leader of the Opposition, from attending official functions in honour of Reagan. C.J. was deprived of an official seat in Galway; attempts were made to exclude him from meeting Reagan in Dail Eireann; and a final rather juvenile effort was made to deprive him of seeing off Reagan at Dublin Airport. Each attempt fixated the media on what would happen next. Soon everyone waited for Charlie's next appearance. The whole ridiculous episode only served to reduce the statesman image of Garret Fitzgerald. Reagan was subsequently elected President of the United States for a second term.

Soon after the Reagan fanfare, politics settled down to "normal" in Ireland. The Fianna Fail Parliamentary Party at a routine meeting decided unanimously that the leader of the Party or someone designated by him, should speak on sensitive issues, for example, the political situation in North-East Ireland. The New Ireland Forum Report examined in some detail the various options regarding the future type of government desirable in North-East

Ireland. The only proposal that all the constitutional parties agreed on was that of a unitary state. Desmond O'Malley felt otherwise and as a member of the parliamentary party raised his point of view at the parliamentary party meeting. He failed to gain a consensus of opinion for his point of view and the parliamentary party unanimously declared that it would stand by the New Ireland Forum Report. O'Malley persisted with his opinion and the parliamentary party was left with no option but to remove the whip from him. The February 1985 vote on the Contraceptives Bill saw O'Malley vote contrary to his party, Fianna Fail. The issue had to be resolved once and for all. It is clearly impossible for a party leader to operate effectively if he cannot count on the parliamentary support of all elected party members. On 26 February 1985, Desmond O'Malley was expelled from Fianna Fail. Charles Haughey was again blamed for O'Malley's political mistakes. Others said that O'Malley would get over 30% support of the total voting public in Ireland, but events in his career have shown that O'Malley usually faltered at the critical moment. The O'Malley debacle was of considerable interest to Fine Gael. They would have gained from any weakness or problem in Fianna Fail. The Labour Party were in a weak position in government. Their former leader Michael O'Leary was quick to realise this when he jumped ship to Fine Gael.

Rank and file members of Fianna Fail were delighted that some real discipline was being restored to the Party. Too many elected T.Ds were whining about the leadership and voting their own way on important public matters. The expulsion of Desmond O'Malley marked the return to a powerful and well-disciplined Parliamentary Party. In November 1985, a Fianna Fail T.D., Mary Harney, sought some publicity for herself. She decided to vote against her Party in the aftermath of the so-called Anglo-Irish Agreement. When she was correctly and democratically expelled from the Party, she went whining off to the sidelines looking for sympathy. It had taken great courage and much effort on the part of Charles Haughey to build the Fianna Fail Parliamentary Party into an Opposition of mature members. Nothing less would suffice if Fianna Fail were to return to govern the country once more.

In 1949 the British War Cabinet noted the following: "Now that Eire will shortly cease to owe any allegiance to the Crown, it has become a matter of first-class strategic importance to this country that the North should continue to form part of His Majesty's dominions . . ." Charles J. Haughey has done much in his time to raise the consciousness of the Irish people. Historically, there has been a tendency to a slave mentality among the Irish where the English are concerned. In earlier times the English landlords had virtually the power of life and death over the native Irish. To this day the British cultivate a subservient mentality among the Irish people and their political representatives.

If the general public in Ireland were presented with the real facts, policies and decision making would have different outcomes. Certainly, very few people in Ireland wish to see the country stacked high with an endless variety of nuclear weapons. We have already a sophisticated array of devices for tracking satellites and missiles, devices for listening to underwater noises, devices for the detection of water turbulence from the propellors of nuclear submarines and undoubtedly a number of other such instruments which are still highly secret. It is all naturally for our own good and for our protection.

The huge expenditure on so-called Border security goes unheeded. The 1986 gross expenditure for Security in the Republic of Ireland is estimated at £661 million or 4% of gross national product (G.N.P.). Border security involves a large number of gardai, patrol cars, barrack facilities with battalions of troops operating from Finner Camp, Monaghan Barracks, Castleblaney and Dundalk Barracks with immediate back up from Gormanstown Camp and the huge Curragh complex. It is relatively easy to assume that a figure of £150 million per annum on Border security is correct. Britain has approximately 15 times the population of the Republic of Ireland. Their Border security expenditure, to match proportionately that of Ireland, should be in the region of £2,250 million. It is nowhere near that figure. It is in the order of some £200 million. To match Britain proportionately, Ireland should spend 15 times less or approximately £13 million. The £137 million saved would provide a sizeable amount of funds to curb lawlessness in the larger towns and cities. The exactness of the above figures may be disputed, but it is an irrefutable fact that we are spending far in excess of what should be spent on so-called Border security. To add insult to injury, we have the spectacle of the Chief Constable of the R.U.C, Jack Hermon deriding us for our lack of commitment to security and in some well documented cases, even trying to put the blame on the Gardai when breaches of security occurred in his territory. Why do we accept this ludicrous situation as normal?

Charles Haughey has never accepted foreign interference in Irish affairs. He has continuously exhorted the people of Ireland to stand up and be proud of their nation and of its achievements in the 20th century. He has on several occasions stated unequivocally that the six counties (Derry, Antrim, Down, Armagh, Tyrone and Fermanagh) of North-East Ireland belong to the people of Ireland and as such, should be governed by the elected representatives of the people of Ireland. Since the other 26 counties of Ireland wrested their independence from Britain early in the 20th century, there has been no persecution of the inhabitants on religious or political grounds. Citizens in the Republic of Ireland have the right to practise their own religion coupled with the right to vote for their preferred party at regular, democratic elections. Catholics, Protestants, Jews and Agnostics have been associated with, and participated in, public life in Ireland. When the six counties of North-East Ireland are integrated into the Republic, every citizen of that region will retain the right to practise his religion along with his right to vote. Elected representatives from North-East Ireland will have the right to sit in Dail Eireann and fully represent their constituents. After all, the inhabitants of North-East Ireland are Irish men and Irish women, as are the inhabitants of the Republic. Much urging will be needed to persuade Britain and its rulers to let go of the six North-Eastern counties of Ireland. The fact that Ireland and Britain are both members of the E.E.C. is already a major step in breaking down the barriers and differences of opinion between the two countries on the problem of "Northern Ireland".

The New Ireland Forum commenced its deliberations on 30 May 1983. The Forum attempted to bring a ray of hope and another opportunity to talk and to determine a peaceful and acceptable resolution to the current political impasse in North-East Ireland. In his speech at the opening of the Forum, Charles Haughey said:

Today is an historic occasion. For the first time in sixty years political parties North and South, who support the restoration of Irish unity by peaceful means, have come together to determine what new political structures are needed to achieve peace and stability on this island. Our purpose is to construct a basic position, which can then be put to an all-round constitutional conference, convened by the Irish and British Governments as a prelude to British withdrawal. The parties gathered here represent a weight of opinion that cannot easily be ignored or dismissed. Together they represent the overwhelming majority of Nationalist opinion on this island, and a clear majority of the Irish people as a whole.

Early in this century a great unified effort was required to secure independence in the greater part of this island. A similar concerted effort is now required to finally secure an end to the tragic problem that Northern Ireland represents today.

Despite the impressive membership and the historic surroundings, this Forum will only succeed in its political objectives, if we recognise the realities. Our work must be informed by a clear understanding of the problems if it is to lead to a permanent solution.

The first of these realities is that peace and stability cannot be secured without a withdrawal of the British military and political presence from Northern Ireland as the Minister for Foreign Affairs has recently emphasised. In saying this we are neither diminishing the importance of any other aspect or denying the need to safeguard and protect the Northern Unionist population. Anyone who stands back from the situation can see clearly that it is the British military and political presence which distorts the situation in Northern Ireland and inhibits the normal process by which peace and stability emerge elsewhere. That process can only develop and peace and stability be secured under new all-Ireland structures in the context of which an orderly British withdrawal can take place.

The present situation in Northern Ireland is not primarily the fault of anyone living there. It is the cumulative effect of British policy in Ireland over many hundreds of years; a fact which any British Government which wishes to solve the problem must start by recognising.

It is common ground amongst us in this Forum that we are prepared to work in close cooperation with any British Government to bring forward a solution to a problem that continuously distorts Anglo-Irish relations and relations within this island because no British Government will be able to provide any solution to the problem other than in partnership with the Irish Government.

The concept of a Council for a new Ireland which gave rise to this New Ireland Forum arose out of the political circumstances of last year. In the face of an unacceptable British Government initiative, which placed the political representatives of the Nationalist community in Northern Ireland in an impossible position, some alternative action was needed. The Nationalist people in Northern Ireland could not accept that there was no further useful role for Nationalist constitutional politics. This Forum was conceived as an alternative to a total stalemate.

The British Government cannot be allowed to play the role of disinterested peacemaker between warring factions. Britain is in fact, whether she recognises it or not acting in a partisan role, supporting unconditionally the basic Unionist position, by military, political and economic power. The present Northern Ireland Assembly, a Unionist-dominated body, has been explicitly stated by the Secretary of State for Northern Ireland to be designed to tie Northern Ireland into the United Kingdom forever.

The parties represented here today have come together on the basis of a common purpose. We believe, first of all, that it is only in the context of Irish unity that a lasting solution to the Northern Ireland problem can be found and, secondly, that Irish unity can only come about by the use of constitutional political means.

Northern Ireland was founded on the threat of civil war and has rested ever since on an unhappy foundation of civil and military power. Thirteen years of violence and 2,000 deaths have brought sorrow, bitterness and frustration.

The British Army, sent in 1969 to pacify the province and uphold the constitutional position, has manifestly failed in its task.

Perhaps its task was impossible anyhow and the repression of the civilian population that has taken place inevitable. The paramilitary organisations have nothing to show either but a legacy of hatred and suspicion.

Partition was brought forward over sixty years ago to solve a political problem but has totally failed to do so over that long period. Another political solution must now be found.

Ulster has long played a pivotal role in Irish life. From Ulster christian missionaries went forth to Scotland, and St. Columba's island of Iona symbolises the link between all the people of these islands.

The siege of Derry and the battle of the Boyne, the birth of Republicanism among the Presbyterians of Belfast, the meeting of the Irish Volunteers in Dungannon—these and many other events had a profound effect on the course of Irish history. Modern Ireland reflects these events and happenings and while Ulster has often been the scene of conflict and antagonisms it has also been a source of courage, inspiration and patriotism.

The discussions in the New Ireland Forum must be founded on respect for the Unionist tradition, but also and equally on respect for our own. In Ireland today we all are what we are: we must accept each other as we are, neither apologising nor condemning, but working to find solutions on the basis of mutual tolerance and acceptance. What independent Ireland has built up over the last sixty years is the natural foundation of the new Ireland but we do not see unity in terms of the people of the North being absorbed into or annexed by the Republic. It is instead a question of building the new Ireland with their help and participation, using the materials that we have both North and South, benefitting from our respective experience and the institutions that we have developed.

The new Ireland must be firmly based on agreement and consent. There have been attempts to create a confusion and misunderstanding as to what this would mean from those living in the South. The belief has been canvassed that we would have to jettison almost the entire ethos on which the independence movement was built and that the Irish identity has to be sacrificed to facilitate the achievement of Irish unity. Nothing could be more erroneous or destructive.

In this part of Ireland we have much to be proud of in what has been achieved since independence. We need apologise to nobody about the character or performance of our State, and we do not intend to do so. Independent Ireland was founded on the ideal that all the children of the nation would be cherished equally and in broad measure we have been faithful to that ideal, particularly in respect of political and religious minorities. If there have been blemishes, they are small ones and not necessarily all on the one side.

The challenge is to find a way of accommodating our different strongly held beliefs and cultural values, rather than to supress or supplant one by another. We accept without reservation the right of the people of Northern Ireland to retain the way of life to which they are accustomed and to the full expression of their identity and their beliefs.

Agreement and consent means that the political arrangements in Ireland to be established following the cessation of the British military and political presence will have to be negotiated, agreed and consented to by the people of Ireland, North and South, or by their political representatives acting on their behalf.

Partition, the State of Northern Ireland itself, was never legitimate from a democratic point of view and cannot be made so. But we readily and willingly concede that the establishment of a new political order in Ireland and a new social contract can only come about through a major revision of existing structures.

I believe that a new constitution will be required for a new Ireland. A united Ireland would represent a constitutional change of such magnitude as to demand a new constitution. That constitution in our view, can only be formulated at an all-round constitutional conference in which all sections of the Irish people North and South would participate. It is only in this way that we can provide all the appropriate safeguards and guarantees required for the security and protection of every section of the Irish community.

The divergent practice which has been followed in many matters, not just matters of a conscientious or moral nature, North and South, means that complete harmonisation of laws, administrative practices and social structures may only be possible, if carried out over a gradual and perhaps extended period. We may have to consider some degree of autonomy for Northern Ireland, be it on the basis of the same area, or a smaller one. We have the example, in the state of Great Britain for instance, of Scotland with its own legal system and its own educational system, an administration in

Edinburgh, a Cabinet minister, and a grand committee of Scottish M.P.s in Westminister who legislate on Scottish affairs.

Eamon de Valera's offer in 1938 which would have allowed for the continuation of a subsidiary parliament, was based on the principle that sovereignty would be transferred from Britain to Ireland, but that Northern Ireland would continue to enjoy the autonomy it possessed at that time. How relevant that concept is today must be considered in the light of all that has happened since and in particular the fact that in 1972 the Government and Parliament of Northern Ireland were abolished, in recognition of the fact that the State of Northern Ireland could no longer function as a political entity.

Our deliberations must have regard to the practical considerations militating against the setting up of two, or possibly three, governments and parliaments in this small island whether they are in a relationship of equality or subordination to each other. Ireland is too small to need or support elaborate tiers of Government.

We shall, I hope, look with open minds on a variety of different political structures. We would greatly wish to have full Northern participation in an Irish Government and Parliament from the beginning. At present, Northern politicians play no direct role in the government of Northern Ireland. From that frustration there naturally arises a fear among Unionists that in a new Ireland they might also be without power or influence and the people they represent discriminated against.

A proposal which must be maturely examined is that for a specified transitional period power should be shared in the island as a whole. In an extended and reconstituted Government for the whole island, arrangements could be devised to guarantee adequate participation in government by Northern representatives.

A matter of equal importance is the status of Ireland's relations with Britain and with other countries. A new Ireland would be a sovereign independent state: the Irish Republic desired by generations since the day of the first Belfast republicans of the late 18th century. That Republic could develop structures, relationships, associations of a bilateral or multilateral kind with Britain that would not compromise our sovereignty and independence, but would give recognition to the long established links with Britain of those who adhere to the Unionist tradition in Ireland.

It goes without saying that no one possessing British citizenship would be deprived of it and it ought to be possible to negotiate for the continuation and passing on of such citizenship rights to those who valued them.

We recognize that Britain has her own defence requirements. In this Forum we shall advocate the principle already stated that Ireland would never allow her territory to be used as a base for attack on Britain and would be prepared to enter into a treaty arrangement needed for that purpose.

This Forum will necessarily concentrate much of its attention on the economic implications of unity.

As a general principle there is no reason why this whole island with all its known resources and those still to be explored should not develop to the same level of material prosperity as has been reached anywhere else in Europe.

The establishment of a lasting peace in Ireland would bring very considerable economic benefits to both parts of Ireland, some of them immediately, others in the long-term. The whole island, but particularly Northern Ireland, would become a much more attractive location for investment. The tourist industry would revive immediately and dramatically. The heavy burden of security would be greatly reduced.

Joining the two parts of Ireland together would produce economies of scale and open up a variety of possibilities for advantageous cooperation. The enlargement of the domestic market for both parts of Ireland would be a major benefit in itself. Joint investment, export and tourism promotion programmes would bring benefits to the whole island, and would give Northern Ireland the benefit of access to what are universally acknowledged as successful State agencies in the South. Cooperation in transport and communications; in developing our agricultural structures and markets would bring immediate and substantial benefits.

In economic and political terms as a nation of five million people we would be a country comparable in size and international status with many of the Scandinavian countries such as Denmark, Norway or Finland. The interests of both parts of the country could be more effectively promoted from this unified base. At present the voice of Northern Ireland is scarcely heard at all, overshadowed as it is by that of London. This Forum should be able to demonstrate to the political representatives of Northern Ireland that sharing in the leadership of this country and of this island, and having a voice in international Councils, is infinitely preferable to continuing in a kind of political limbo that is their position at present.

There can be no longer any doubt left in anyone's mind about the desire in the nationalist philosophy to promote the economic welfare of this island as a whole North and South. The Republic has offered Kinsale gas to the North on reasonable terms; we subsidise the Dublin/Derry air service. We are pursuing actively the possibility of arranging for engineering and shipbuilding contracts to go northward. The one Member of the European Parliament representing the National community of Northern Ireland has diligently sought to promote the economic welfare of Northern Ireland right across the board in Brussels and has had the whole-hearted support of his Southern colleagues in his efforts.

We can, I suggest, envisage an economic transitional period of reasonable length between the new Ireland and the old. It would be reasonable to request the British Government to make a major contribution to assisting the transition by economic and financial measures.

There would almost certainly be a willingness in the European community to contribute to investment in economic infrastructure and firm indications have already been given of U.S. willingness to participate in the economic development of a united Ireland.

This New Ireland Forum, if we adhere to clear objectives, can certainly mark a new phase in progress towards a lasting and peaceful solution throughout Ireland. This time last year we celebrated the bicentenary of Grattan's Parliament and the declaration of independence of 1782. The national unity of 1782 was all too brief a moment of exhilaration but like other movements in Irish history it inspired many succeeding generations.

It was here in Dublin Castle, two and a half years ago, that a British Prime Minister acknowledged that the problem of Northern Ireland could be solved by joint action of the two sovereign Governments. It is with that truth clearly in our minds that this

Forum takes the first steps along the road to a final constitutional settlement.

Unionist and Nationalist, Protestant and Catholic all share the one island, and are deeply attached to its soil. All belong and have a contribution to make to our common country. We may not have chosen one another as neighbours, but it is as neighbours we have to live. Nobody else can settle for us the problems we have or think we have as neighbours. We have to solve them together or they will remain unsolved with all the cost in material terms and human suffering that this will entail.

The time is ripe for a new start. It is our duty to rekindle the spirit and the political energies of the nation. The people of the North, as part of the people of Ireland, have a long tradition of resilience and courage, which in the past has been put to the service of Ireland. The descendants of those that led this nation in the past, the United Irishmen of the North who made the mental break with the British connection and who thereby altered the whole mould of Irish history, not merely have a future on this island, but are in a position to help guide its destinies. The pride of the people of the North in their province, in what they have painstakingly built, is a virtue that we admire. They have now, as they had before, an opportunity to help lead a country of five million people, and to take a place of honour in its Government. This surely is preferable to being a neglected offshore annex of the island of Great Britain.

I am certain that ways can be found of reconciling even our most fundamental aspirations, and that by coming together we can create a prosperity which will elude us so long as we remain divided.

We seek to broaden the base of the society that is founded upon the Irish nation with equal treatment for all, in which there will be no domination or exploitation of particular groups, communities or regions. When we finally come together, we will enjoy the support and encouragement of friendly nations, who will gladly welcome the healing of our divisions.

Reconciliation needs the support of political structures. Aspirations and platitudes are not enough. It will only be through new political structures in a new political context that the reconciliation of the different Irish traditions will be achieved, without loss of identity or abandonment of old loyalties, and in which all traditions will find their representation as of right. These new structures if they are wisely planned will enable us to banish discrimination, bias and confrontation from Ireland forever—an objective which surely merits our best endeavours and total commitment.

At the Fianna Fail Ard-Fheis in March 1985, Charles Haughey set out once again the view of Fianna Fail and that of the majority of the people living on the island of Ireland. An extract from his speech on that occasion states:

"In our view the way forward and the objective on which the Irish Government should concentrate and to which it should devote all its political and diplomatic efforts is persuading the British Government to convene an all round constitutional conference as set out in the Forum report for the purpose of preparing constitutional structures for a new unitary state embracing the whole island of Ireland. It is only in this constitutional context that the Irish people of all traditions will achieve their full potential and that bitterness, civil strife and the animosity of centuries will be finally laid to rest."

On 13 May 1945, Churchill, the British Prime Minister, made a major speech attacking De Valera who had just successfully steered Ireland on a neutral course through the horrors of World War II. Thinking that he was funny and original, he insisted on pronouncing De Valera's name as "Devil Eire". In the part of his speech referring to Ireland, Churchill siad:

". . . Owing to the action of Mr. De Valera, so much at variance with the temper and instinct of thousands of southern Irishmen, who hastened to the battlefront to prove their ancient valour, the approaches which the southern Irish ports and airfields could so easily have guarded were closed by the hostile aircraft and U-boats.

"This was indeed a deadly moment in our life, and if it had not been for the loyalty and friendship of Northern Ireland, we should have been forced to come to close quarters with Mr. De Valera, or perish for ever from the earth. However, with a restraint and poise, to which I venture to say history will find few parallels, H.M. Government never laid a violent hand upon them, though at times it would have been quite easy and quite natural, and we left the De

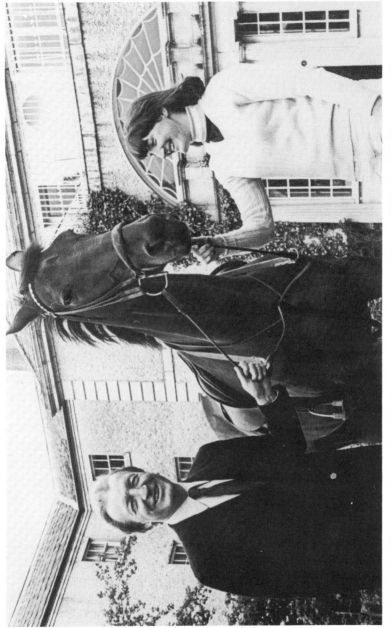

With daughter Eimear and a mutual friend. Eimear is an accomplished rider, well liked and highly respected in equestrian circles.

Valera Government to frolic with the German and later with the Japanese representatives to their heart's content."

Three days later, on 16 May 1945, De Valera went on radio to reply to Churchill. Everyone expected a tirade, but his speech was masterful. He said he knew what many people were expecting him to say and what he would have said 25 years earlier, but the occasion now demanded something else. He explained that Churchill could be excused for being carried away in the excitement of victory, but there would be no such excuse for himself. Speaking calmly the Taoiseach said:

"Mr. Churchill makes it clear that, in certain circumstances, he would have violated our neutrality and that he would justify his action by Britain's necessity. It seems strange to me that Mr. Churchill does not see that this, if it be accepted, would mean that Britain's necessity would become a moral code and that, when this necessity became sufficiently great, other people's rights were not to count. It is quite true that other great powers believe in this same code — in their own regard — and have behaved in accordance with it. This is precisely why we have the disastrous succession of wars — World War No. 1 and World War No. 2 — and shall it be World War No. 3?" Then with magnificent audacity he turned to praise Churchill for resisting the temptation to violate Irish neutrality:

"It is, indeed, hard for the strong to be just to the weak. But acting justly always has its rewards. By resisting his temptation in this instance, Mr. Churchill, instead of adding another horrid chapter to the already bloodstained record of relations between England and this country, has advanced the cause of international morality an important step . . ."

De Valera's broadcast caused a sensation in Ireland and abroad. It subsequently went down in history as his finest speech ever. Do we still value our neutrality? Since that famous speech of De Valera, the world has become a smaller place to live in. Ballistic missiles can travel for thousands of miles and "accurately" knock out military targets. Will we survive as neutrals or will a future British government under severe pressure grab our airports and vital installations and fight part of a short, vicious and devastating Third World War from our territory?

At the Fianna Fail Ard-Fheis of March 1985, Charles Haughey had this to say on Irish neutrality:

"Neutrality is a principle of our foreign policy which the great majority of Irish people want their Government to maintain whatever the pressures from any quarter. Any departure from that position will inevitably involve us in the nuclear strategy of existing alliances and pressure for the provision of nuclear facilities in this country. Fianna Fail are resolved to preserve the whole of Ireland as a nuclear-free zone, and we see clearly that this is only possible on the basis of maintaining our military neutrality."

*   *   *

On 1 May 1985, the Taoiseach Garret Fitzgerald departed Ireland for an extended 12 day visit to the North American Continent. Nobody was really sure about why he was undertaking this tour or what was the purpose of it. It was said that he was going to raise American business investment in Ireland; to debate international affairs; to raise international consciousness about the Forum Report, the North of Ireland, the Anglo-Irish talks; to give some lectures; to collect an honorary degree at St. Mary's University in Halifax, Nova Scotia; to speak on the situation in Lebanon; to attend a weird secret "Bilderberg" conference. The whole visit turned into an indecisive muddle of fumbling uncertainty, secrecy and contradiction. When Charles Haughey, leader of the Opposition, asked the relevant question, "What's he doing out there anyway!", a multitude of answers floated across the Atlantic. By their variety and multiplicity, the average citizen was more puzzled than ever. Much time has passed and we still don't know who attended that secret Bilderberg conference in New York or what was on the agenda or even if there was an agenda. The book, *"Trilateralism: The Trilateral Commission and Elite Planning for World Management"*, edited by Holly Sklar, South End Press, Boston, 1980, does provide some guidelines. Four sentences quoted from the book serve to illustrate the secrecy surrounding each conference.

"The object is not to 'draw the attention' of the greater population to Bilderberg activity. Bilderberg's existence is often denied, even by foreign ministry officials. Apart from planted newspaper articles, no Bilderberg publications are available to the public. The extent of media blackout is remarkable."

Was it fair to hide the deliberations of such a conference from the media in particular when Dr. Fitzgerald speaks as Taoiseach in the name of the people of Ireland?

On 20 June 1985, a little over a month after the U.S. tour of Dr. Fitzgerald, local elections were held in Ireland. They ended in countrywide resounding victories for Charles Haughey and Fianna Fail. After thirty months in office Fine Gael and Labour won only 37.5% compared with 48.6% in November 1982. This represented a significant drop of just over 11%. Fianna Fail had an outstanding performance in Dublin city and county where just under 30% of the total Dail seats are located. After a long spell in a minority position, Fianna Fail could once again elect a Lord Mayor of Dublin, Jim Tunney T.D. and a Chairman of Dublin County Council, Ray Burke T.D. The Labour vote continued to slide in the Dublin City electoral area. They found themselves in fourth place behind The Workers Party. The election victories of Fianna Fail can only be attributed to good strategy and planning on the part of its leader and public representatives. While Charles Haughey has demonstrated his decisiveness and ability to lead, the Coalition Government have been wrestling with national problems for over three years. The working citizen sees his salary decreasing in real value terms and the unemployed see little prospect of salary or wages in the foreseeable future. When the Local Results were known, Charles Haughey said:

"The people want a general election now. They want a change of government and they want a change of policy. But I can't get rid of the government until such time as the Labour Party ministers who have taken the Fine Gael shilling come to their senses and realise that they are destroying not only the Labour Party but the country as well. This was a magnificent victory for Fianna Fail both nationally and especially in Dublin city and county. Not since the party was founded have we been in such a good position in Dublin city and county."

The memorable election victory proved beyond all doubt that

Charles Haughey has the ability, enthusiasm and flair to win elections and to lead the Irish people into a better future now so ardently desired.

* * *

It would be difficult if not impossible to select a round of talks or a deal where Britain actually did something which would be of benefit to Ireland. In the recent past British action on the Milk Levy was to Ireland's disadvantage. Perhaps the most blatant of all was when Mrs. Thatcher, the British Prime Minister, realised that the Kinsale gas pipeline to North-East Ireland would actually benefit the Irish economy. The proposed pipeline was immediately scrapped. Irish leaders who negotiate with Britain about anything, should be very circumspect. The history of negotiations with Britain in the 20th century is one of bad deals for Ireland. The Border Security payment is perhaps one of the worst. It represents an ongoing expenditure which is out of all proportion to that spent by Britain on security in the North-East sector of Ireland. A new Agreement has been signed at Hillsborough, Co. Down. Time will tell what the cost will be to the Irish taxpayer. One thing is certain—it will cost the Irish taxpayer far more than his British counterpart.

It would be foolish to think that by the act of signing the Hillsborough Agreement, Britain has begun to contemplate the evacuation of North-East Ireland. To my knowledge Britain has never withdrawn her military occupation of a country through the simple signing of a paper agreement. There has usually been strife and bloodshed. Since 1969, the North-East sector of Ireland has witnessed a period of sustained strife and bloodshed. There have been paper understandings and agreements, but in 1986, the strife and bloodshed continues.

Since November 1982, Charles Haughey has led what must be the strongest opposition to any government in the history of the State. He has tried hard to prevent Garret Fitzgerald from putting his foot in it at regular intervals. We do not need to be reminded of the 18% VAT on children's clothes and footwear or the rapidly deteriorating financial situation of the average citizen of Ireland. The disastrous

18% VAT Budget of 27 January 1982 caused the fall of the Coalition Government. Fitzgerald cannot say that he was not warned in advance, yet he once again put numbers in front of people. It was just a continuation of his custom of putting book balancing before the genuine needs of people. The same can never be said of Charles Haughey. He has always made time to listen to the humblest citizen. His enlightened legislation over the years has been enacted to the ultimate benefit of the ordinary citizen.

We now come to the Agreement promoted as the one to end all agreements—the so-called Anglo-Irish Document signed in two originals at Hillsborough, Co. Down on 15 November 1985. This Agreement has diluted the original ideal of a Unitary State as envisioned by Michael Collins and Eamon De Valera in the 1920s. Charles J. Haughey and Fianna Fail were correct in opposing the Agreement. It is the duty of the Opposition to point out the flaws in Government decisions. It has been demonstrated over and over again that Garret Fitzgerald has a strong tendency to overlook the obvious and blunder on until someone calls him to a halt. Remember the Bilderberg secret conference attended by him in his capacity as the representative of the people of Ireland! However well meaning his intentions were, when he signed the Hillsborough Agreement in November '85, time will once more prove that Ireland will come out of it second best. All historical agreements and understandings between the two countries have ultimately favoured Britain. The November '85 Agreement will prove to be no different. The bulky document looks good at first swift perusal. The central theme from the British point of view is that the Republic will assume limited responsibility for what is happening in North-East Ireland. The Republic will have no real say in the running of the sector. If the British want a collection of nuclear missiles stationed less than 100 miles from Dublin, there is nothing that the Republic can do about it. Margaret Thatcher, Prime Minister of Britain, decided to fight a vicious war against Argentina. If she or a future British Prime Minister decide to fight a war against a country with nuclear weapons, is the Republic of Ireland going to be spared?

In the aftermath of the signing of the Hillsborough Agreement, Charles Haughey is blamed for the exit of a Fianna Fail T.D. The truth was that Mary Harney, an adult T.D., made up her own mind that she would not adhere to Party regulations. A parting of the ways was the obvious solution. As an independent T.D. she is now free to say what she pleases, whenever she pleases and to whomsoever she pleases. In the recent past Garret Fitzgerald silenced Oliver J. Flanagan, Tom O'Donnell and Alice Glenn. There was no vociferous public outcry against him. In November 1985, he quietly removed the excommunication edict and received the conscience-stricken trio back into the Party fold without even the requirement of a promise not to commit the sin again. The event passed almost unnoticed by everyone.

On 3 December 1985, less than three weeks after the signing of the Hillsborough Agreement, the worst fears of Charles Haughey came true. The Northern Secretary, Tom King attended a lunch in Brussels hosted by the British Ambassador. During the course of the lunch he decided to make a "surprise" statement which included the following quotation:

"In Northern Ireland now," he said, "we have signed an agreement in which the Prime Minister of Ireland, notwithstanding the fact that he faces and has to live with a Constitution which has aspirations of sovereignty over Northern Ireland, has in fact accepted that for all practical purposes and into perpetuity, there will not be a united Ireland because he has accepted the principle of consent that the will of the majority in Northern Ireland must predominate and that Northern Ireland, which is our fervent wish, remains part of the United Kingdom."

Later Mr. King said in response to questions: "What has been widely misunderstood about this agreement is that it marks the acceptance in a formal agreement, which will be lodged as a treaty at the United Nations by the Government of the Republic, of the principle of consent. Therefore, the legitimacy of the Unionist position based on the majority view in Northern Ireland is accepted, and that therefore means that, as you put it, for all practical purposes, there is no prospect of a united Ireland.

"What I sought to say in the agreement as well is, that being the situation, and that being recognised by the Government of the Republic, it is right also that the minority who do not identify with the United Kingdom but who'll now have to accept that this is going to be the position, that they have to have an opportunity, a proper opportunity, in which to have confidence that their views are taken into account, not that they can dominate, because obviously the views of the majority are very important in this matter, but at least their views are taken into account before decisions are taken by UK Ministers."

Garret Fitzgerald was reported as being hurt, embarrassed, angry and baffled by the luncheon utterances of Tom King. He should not have been. Many, many citizens of Ireland could have told him that Britain has no intention now or in the foreseeable future, of releasing the six north-eastern counties into the jurisdiction of the Irish 26 county Republic. Although Garret Fitzgerald may think that Tom King's remarks were singularly inappropriate and inaccurate, they came from the heart. Tom King was perhaps a little unwise to express publicly what he knew to be the truth privately.

CHAPTER 5

INTERESTING EPHEMERA

The debate on the electricity Supply Amendment Bill concluded in March 1985. The "enormous ugliness" of the huge pylons and overhead supply lines bringing electricity from the new Moneypoint Power Station on the West coast to the East coast, was criticised by Mr. Haughey during the debate on the committee stage of the above Bill. He said:

"These great big gangling pylons seem to march across the countryside like an invading army of martians. They are marching in a dead straight line from Moneypoint to Dublin, up hill and down dale, across valleys, through woodlands without any regard whatever to their visual impact on the countryside."

He also stated that Moneypoint power station was a doubtful economic proposition and he asked the Tanaiste and Minister for Energy, Dick Spring, was he alert to the position about atmospheric pollution from the plant. There was the distinct possibility that some of the rare and unique plant life of the Burren district in Co. Clare could be destroyed or seriously damaged. The Tanaiste assured Mr. Haughey that emissions would be closely monitored. It is estimated that emissions of the deadly pollutant known as Sulphur Dioxide will continuously sweep across Ireland driven by the prevailing South Westerly winds. An estimated 70,000 tons of this well documented pollutant will fall softly and silently on Irish soil every year. Perhaps by the time you read these words, the E.S.B. will have declared the Moneypoint Power Station free of dangerous emissions. At the present time, a silent killer is sweeping through the forests of Northern Europe. It comes in the form of "acid rain", the result of atmospheric pollution by large industries who do not properly detoxify their deadly emissions. The year 2000 AD will have witnessed the death of a large variety of arborial and other vegetative life on the European continent. It is to be fervently hoped that Ireland will not become a contributor to the mass destruction of our European natural heritage. Other voices will have to speak out and follow the example and the concern of Charles J. Haughey for all things natural and beautiful.

The Eire Society in America seeks to promote the knowledge of Irish culture abroad. It awards an annual gold medal to individuals who have made an outstanding contribution in the arts, sciences, literature, language, history or government in an Irish context. In April 1985, Charles Haughey was the recipient of the Eire Society Gold Medal for his significant contribution to the promotion of all things Irish. The presentation took place at the Park Plaza Hotel in Boston.

Speaking to the Waterford Chamber of Commerce on 11 October 1985, Charles Haughey called for the development of a cheap energy economy based on natural gas. He said:

"I would be prepared to be quite oncoming in the selective use of this natural resource now to generate economic activity and employment and get us out of this present disastrous economic situation."

He added that in face of rising unemployment and high emigration, the country needed a coherent policy for the development of our natural resources. In regard to oil exploration, Fianna Fail would watch any developments carefully to ensure that the exploitation of any oil had a proper balance. Proper use of our natural gas and oil fields could literally fuel our economic recovery. B.P. made a significant gas discovery in the Celtic Sea near the South coast of Ireland in 1985. "There is, by all accounts substantially more gas out there still to be exploited", he concluded.

The white-tailed eagle is a magnificent bird of prey. Also known as the Sea Eagle, it feeds mainly on sea birds such as fulmars, puffins and gulls. It also eats fish and carrion. In 1985 Charles Haughey commissioned a feasibility study to ascertain whether the sea eagle could be introduced to Inismhicileáin and the neighbouring islands. If the various conservation agencies would agree to support him, he would go ahead, he said. Up until the last century, sea eagles were common off the South-West coast of Ireland. By the end of the 19th century they were extinct, having been victims of shooting and poisoning. Inismhicileáin, which has a corner known as the "Eagles Hollow" appears to be ideally suited to these marine birds. There is a huge seabird population in the area assuring a plentiful supply of food if the sea eagles are introduced. One of the major attractions in introducing this bird is the fact that unlike other eagles, it does not attack sheep which are kept extensively along the Kerry coastline.

The sea eagle was successfully introduced to the Scottish Island of Rhum about ten years ago. Although no young were reared yet, it is regarded as a significant fact that the eagles have laid eggs. The possibility of them breeding in the near future is greatly enhanced. Charles Haughey thinks that the Rhum Island eagles are beginning to extend their range as far as the Blasket Islands off the Kerry coast. It would be a novel project for the Irish Wildbird Conservancy and its chances of success are excellent.

In 1985 the Great Blasket island was advertised for sale in the Wall Street Journal. The asking price was 900,000 dollars. Charles Haughey described the island as a literary shrine and declared that everything possible to preserve its traditional character should be done. The Great Blasket was the home of the celebrated Gaelic writers Peig Sayers, Muiris O Suilleabháin and Tomás O Criomhthain. The Great Blasket is situated just six miles from Inismhicileáin where Charles Haughey has a holiday home. The Blasket Islands lie off the South West coast of Kerry.

Mr. Haughey said that, if necessary, special legislation should be enacted in order to acquire the island as a national park. "In my view it is bad enough that the people there were forced by lack of facilities to leave, but at least the island must be preserved in its traditional form," he said.

The chairman of the West Kerry Development Co-operative, an tUas. Tomas MacGearailt, called for the island to be designated as a major heritage centre with the Government initiating a programme to preserve and develop all aspects of its tradition.

"This most westerly land point in Europe is significant because of its location, its archaeology, its natural history, its folklore and of course its great natural beauty," he added.

Statue of Cuchulainn sculpted from a fallen Great Elm at Abbeville.
(Photo: Fionan O'Connell.)

Charles Haughey has compiled an extensive and wide ranging collection of paintings, maps, books and objets d'art at his Abbeville, Kinsaley home. Among his collection of paintings are two depicting the sea coast of Portmarnock/Malahide in North County Dublin by the renowned artist Nathaniel Hone. A large canvas shows hunting hounds and horses following a fox who is escaping across a railway embankment in the face of an oncoming train. It is titled "Narrow Squeak" and was painted by the famous artist Walter Osborne. There are maps which include Rocque's map of the County of Dublin in 1760. Among the numerous paintings, drawings and engravings is a beautiful framed photograph of Eimear, the eldest child and only daughter of Charles and Maureen Haughey.

A rather elegant and exquisitely beautiful statue of Cuchulainn stands under the leafy shade to the front of Abbeville House. It is unique in the fact that it is carved from the trunk of a Great Elm which once grew in the green fields of Abbeville Stud. Charles Haughey discovered it blown down after a particularly severe Winter storm had swept over Kinsaley. He immediately engaged the well known sculptor Joan Smith who transformed the tree into a refined and sensitive work of art.

The lands at Abbeville have been stocked with pheasant and duck. Two white swans are nesting peacefully on the little lake. There is an extensive variety of flora growing in the vicinity of the lake and stream which meanders through the Abbeville lands on its way to the sea at Portmarnock's Velvet Strand. Some of these unique plants and shrubs were introduced to Ireland in the 18th century.

Like most people Charles Haughey has had accidents serious and minor in his lifetime. In August and in September 1985, he was involved in two mishaps which could have ended in tragedy. The first occurred at Farranfore Airport in County Kerry. On landing at the airport, one of the struts supporting the undercarriage developed a defect as the light twin-engined Cessna was taxiing to a halt shortly after noon on 27 August 1985.

A spokesman for Iona Airways said: "The plane made a normal landing and there were no difficulties and no injuries". Mr Haughey was uninjured and continued on to his holiday home on the Blasket island of Inismhicileáin.

The second mishap occurred in the early hours of Sunday 29 September 1985 off a lonely promontory on the South West coast of County Cork. Mizen Head is one of Europe's most significant headlands. It is Ireland's equivalent to England's Land's End and France's Finisterre in Brittany. On sailing from the West, once round the Mizen you are into the calmer waters of the South coast of Ireland. The Mizen can be an extremely dangerous headland in stormy weather. Only the light of the spectacularly sited Mizen lighthouse is there to guide the mariner. The lighthouse is situated on the headland's little cliff island of Cruachan, which is reached by a reinforced concrete bridge which leaps the rock chasm in a single span. In normal visibility the light can be seen for a range of 16 miles. In fog a cannon was fired twice every five minutes. Since the political unrest became more acute in North-East Ireland, it was decided that the storing of explosives in such a remote and unprotected location constituted a potential hazard. The fog signal was discontinued and the explosive charges for the cannon were removed.

On Saturday 28 September 1985 Charles Haughey and his crew of four sailed South from Dingle Bay, Co. Kerry to round the Mizen Head. The sea was calm but as night fell a heavy fog lay over the ocean. Mr. Haughey settled down to sleep in the cabin of the family yacht, Taurima II. Unknown to the crew, the radar developed a fault during the night and soon they were nearly a mile off course and headed for the deadly underwater rocks off Mizen Head. Mr. Haughey takes up the story himself:

"We were sailing from Dingle, taking the boat back to Dublin. Just as we rounded Mizen Head, something happened to the radar and apparently we were off course. There was dense fog and we struck a rock just under the Mizen light and she went down very quickly. We got into a liferaft and waited for the Baltimore lifeboat.

Conditions were quite good, except for very heavy thick fog, and we were going by our radar. There must have been a malfunction in the radar because we should have been about a mile off Mizen. Instead, we struck a rock under the light."

"I was asleep in the cabin and the first I realised we were in danger was when I awoke to hear a shuddering crunching sound. I rushed up on deck to discover that the bow had rammed onto rocks. The boat went down very quickly, in about 10 to 15 minutes. Conor's reaction was immediate. His VHF distress call which got out minutes before the yacht sank was picked up immediately by Valentia Marine Radio and by the keepers on the Mizen light. Within five minutes Valentia Radio alerted the Baltimore and Valentia lifeboats. The Marine Rescue Centre at Shannon was also alerted and a Mayday broadcast alerting all shipping in the area was transmitted. There were five of us on board: myself, my son Conor, Brian Stafford, Paul Devanney and Vivion Nagle from Clonakilty."

"We immediately launched the two small craft. Conor was up front in the rubber dingy using oars and the four of us were in the liferaft being towed behind. We reached a small sheltered narrow cove and we waited there. The lighthouse people were brilliant. When we hit the rock we called them on our VHF and they responded immediately. They came down the rocks towards us and shone lights on us. They kept us informed of the lifeboat's progress. They were fabulous because they had very strong torches which they shone from the rocks out towards the lifeboat. They were a great assistance to the lifeboat. In fact, the lifeboat might have had difficulty finding us if it was not for the lightkeepers on Mizen. We have no idea what caused the problems with the yacht or radar. We seemed to be a mile out in direction. We were taken into Baltimore, where we were very warmly and hospitably looked after. We were all very sad about the boat. She was a lovely old family boat. We had it for a good while and she gave us much pleasure and relaxation. It was very sad to see her go down."

"The rescue services worked 110 per cent. The Baltimore lads were fantastic. They were brilliant. The secretary of Baltimore lifeboat, Mr. Bushe, got the call, mobilised his crew and launched immediately. I suppose from their point of view it was tricky enough coming into us. We were practically in under the Mizen light. They came in without any bother, hauled us aboard, gave us cups of tea and anything we wanted and had us in here in Baltimore in record time. We wouldn't normally be sailing at this time of night. We tried to bring the boat back on previous occasions, and we couldn't make it, with the gales and storms. So this time we had a good weather forecast, everything looked grand, so we decided to go back this time, one way or another.

Unfortunately, that wasn't to be. I don't think this was the worst drama for me. The only thing about it is the loss of the boat. We will miss her terribly. She was a lovely old seaboat, very comfortable, very safe. We spent a lot of time on her. Despite being in a liferaft for three hours, we were quite comfortable because we were in a little cove just sitting there waiting for the lifeboat. The lads on the Mizen kept us informed, step by step, about the approach of the lifeboat. I wouldn't say I was frightened. It all happened so quickly. Naturally we were a bit frightened when the shudder came, but we had to act so quickly that we didn't have time to be frightened. We just had to get on with it and get the liferaft launched and get into it."

As an example of the dedication of the lifeboat men, one of the first things they asked him for, was a new lifeboat, Mr. Haughey recalled with a smile. On the Monday following the rescue, the office at Leinster House and the Fianna Fail Mount Street offices and Abbeville were swamped with telephone calls and greetings wishing the Fianna Fail leader well after his ordeal. The official party spokesman, Mr. P. J. Mara, said the reaction had been quite extraordinary and was indicative of the affection in which Mr. Haughey was held by the plain people of Ireland. He said people had stopped and waved at him in the streets, and everyone seemed to want to talk to him and shake his hand.

*   *   *

Across the Irish Sea from County Down, lie the scenic resorts of Cumbria with their lovely lakes and mountains. The Lake District is rightly called the most beautiful part of England. The pretty rural coast of Cumbria forms the western boundary of a land that is famous in song and in poetry. It is more than unfortunate that the timeless beauty of this lovely land is defiled by a man-made monster. The monster is a nuclear reprocessing plant called Windscale, lately changed to Sellafield. Every day it pumps some 2,000,000 gallons of effluent down a mile and a half of pipeline and into the shallow Irish Sea. The monster was built in 1947 and for nigh on forty years it has added a mixture of uranium, ruthenium, caesium, strontium and plutonium to the bed of the enclosed, shallow and intensely fished Irish Sea.

N

ALTANTIC
OCEAN

SCOTLAND

Belfast

Cumbria

Sellafield

Isle
of
Man

Dundalk

IRELAND

IRISH
SEA

Dublin

ENGLAND

WALES

Diagram showing the location of Sellafield on the coast of Cumbria.

Twenty five well documented leakages of radioactive substances occurred at Sellafield in the past 29 years. There were hundreds of "minor" leakages and accidents of which the general public are unaware. In October 1957, a serious fire swept through one of the towers. It started in a plutonium production reactor and it burned out of control for at least two days. It is conservatively estimated that a massive 20,000 Curies of radioactivity was released into the atmosphere. The lethal cloud of radioactive vapour drifted as far afield as Holland and Germany. It has only recently been revealed that one of the gases released in 1957 was the highly radioactive polonium 210. Two towers were sealed after the fire and will remain sealed into the foreseeable future. It is impossible to remove the molten radioactive material inside.

The production of plutonium ceased after the 1957 fire. Soon afterwards, the plant commenced the separation of plutonium from spent nuclear fuel. Plutonium is also removed from obsolete nuclear warheads so that it can be transferred to new bombs. Plutonium 239 is so deadly that the lethal dose for an individual is one millionth of one gram. It is estimated that over five hundred thousand grams or half a tonne of plutonium lies on the bed of the Irish Sea. As of now, the Irish Sea will be potentially dangerous for at least two hundred thousand years. It has been foolishly stated officially that the radioactive discharge will drop to the seabed and lie there harmlessly. Studies have already shown that the Irish Sea has strong bottom currents which carry sediment great distances. Initial evidence shows that the radioactive sediment is gradually moving northwards along the coast of Scotland and spreading outwards towards the coast of County Down in North-East Ireland. A spokesman for the Cumbrian Environmental Organisation recently stated that:

"We find it incredible that Caesium 137 levels on West Cumbrian beaches exceed those of Bikini Atoll, an area evacuated because of the dangers posed to the Bikini people by the radioactivity present".

This statement was issued after a team of scientists recently discovered three times as much radioactivity on the Cumbrian shore as on Bikini Atoll in the Pacific. Bikini Atoll was a testing site for Hydrogen Bomb explosions.

The Irish National Radiation Monitoring Service of the Nuclear Energy Board have already shown that radioactive contamination is higher on the part of the Irish coastline closest to the Sellafield nuclear processing plant in Cumbria. The highest levels of radiation were found between Carlingford Lough and Belfast Lough. Caesium radiation alone, is between 10 and 100 times higher on the East coast of Ireland than on the West.

In November 1983, some Greenpeace people were sailing off the Cumbrian coast. They happened to come across a highly radioactive slick in the sea. The slick and subsequent beach pollution were caused by the "accidental" discharge of the toxic ruthenium 106. Twenty miles of Cumbrian beaches were so seriously contaminated that the public were advised to stay away. British Nuclear Fuels were fined £10,000. Some of the Greenpeace divers tried to plug the effluent pipe. They were fined over £30,000!!! It is widely known that once a serious leakage of radioactive effluent or mist occurs, it is extremely difficult if not impossible to retrieve or neutralise the contaminants. Public disquiet rose to such a pitch that the British government was forced to appoint a commission to investigate. The chairman was Sir Douglas Black, president of the British Medical Association. Black said that it would require 40 times more radiation to cause leukaemia in local Seascale residents. He relied on a figure of 400 grams of uranium having been released into the atmosphere between 1952 and 1955. On 16 February 1986, the Sunday Times disclosed that twenty Kgs. or 20,000 grams of uranium was the correct figure, i.e. 50 times more than in the Black Report. In spite of the high rate of cancer close to Sellafield, the Black Report stressed that, "an observed association between two factors does not prove a causal relationship". In July 1984, Charles Haughey called the Black Report a "whitewash". He continued: "If there is a high incidence of leukaemia in an area where a nuclear plant is situated, surely to God the obvious interpretation is that the plant was responsible for it. These figures alone would, in my view, justify closing down the plant immediately for further investigation". Seascale is a pleasant little village on the Cumbrian coast. It lies virtually in the shadow of the huge Sellafield complex. The Black Report "discovered" that child leukaemia in Seascale was only four times the national average. It now appears that the Black Report was inaccurate by a factor of 40!!!

Cushendun, a tiny and picturesque village of 700 people, nestles among the foothills of the Antrim Mountains on the north eastern coast of Ireland. Five cases of child leukaemia have been detected in the village. This is ten times the national average. Other localised studies have noticed an increase in cancer related diseases on the East coast of Ireland. A study published in the British Medical Journal in November 1983 showed that six out of 26 pregnant women produced Downs Syndrome babies. The 26 mothers were all schoolgirls at a Dundalk boarding school in 1957. Dundalk, on the East coast of Ireland, is about 120 miles or 190 kilometres from the Sellafield nuclear plant. There is also considerable alarm over the high incidence of Downs Syndrome births in County Donegal in North West Ireland. The occurrences are of such magnitude that a Department of Health team has begun an investigation. It is now known that radioactive traces from the nuclear plant at Sellafield are to be found in seaweed on the East and North coasts of Ireland, in shellfish and fish in the Irish Sea, in fish as far away as Sweden, and in the organs of animals in the Sellafield region. A competent scientific survey of cancer related diseases in Ireland is now urgently required.

Towards the end of January 1986, the Sellafield nuclear plant discharged some 400 kilograms of radioactive waste into the Irish Sea. It claimed that the discharge was not dangerous. Less than two weeks later, on the morning of 5 February 1986, another leakage occurred at Sellafield in which an undisclosed quantity of radioactive plutonium vapour was released into the air. A strong easterly wind was blowing at the time and the airborne pollutants headed straight for Ireland. The Department of Energy and the Nuclear Energy Board in Dublin said that they were satisfied there was no public danger following assurances from the British Department of the Environment. That submissive statement from Dublin should be kept in mind by the citizens of Ireland. It can be recalled in the light of future events. Initially a spokesman for British Nuclear Fuels, who operate the plant at Sellafield, stated that nobody was contaminated in the 5 February leakage. Later the company admitted to two. A week later it emerged that eleven

Tadhg Kennedy with Charles Haughey discussing the latest disturbing news on radioactive emissions from the nuclear processing plant at Sellafield. *(Photo: Fionan O'Connell.)*

workers received doses of radiation, one so seriously that he will have to work away from the plant for a considerable period. Such blatant lying on the part of British Nuclear Fuels is inexcusable. How many other serious leakages of radioactive effluents and vapours have they lied about in the past? On 13 February 1986, just eight days after the previous accident at Sellafield, a fire broke out in the nuclear dump at Drigg operated by the plant. The public, British and Irish, are assured that tests on smoke samples taken near the fire indicated no significant increase in radioactivity. The fact that a fire could occur so easily in a nuclear dump, of itself indicated a serious lack of safety.

The nuclear dump is a two square mile area of fir treees cordoned off by a three metre high metal fence topped with barbed wire. It is situated about four miles South of Sellafield near the river Irt. Low-level radioactive materials are buried there, in trenches ten metres deep. A tiny stream flows through the dumping area to join the Irt which in turn flows into the sea at Ravenglass. The level of radiation in the stream water is about 100 times that of normal background radiation. The Ravenglass bird sanctuary is situated here. It is a well known nesting place for blackheaded gulls dating back to Roman times in Britain. In the 1960s almost 20,000 pairs of gulls nested here. In the early 1980s only 2,000 pairs remained. In 1986, no blackheaded gull nested in Ravenglass. The "dumb" birds know that something is seriously wrong in the area and have decided to get out while they can. Intelligent humans continue to work and eat and rear their young there. Of course nobody has yet discovered why the gulls have abandoned their historic nesting place at Ravenglass.

On 18 February 1986, yet another spillage of contaminated water occurred. A fractured pipe was blamed this time. Again everyone was assured that there was no significant increase in radioactivity. The hazard to life is now regarded as being so serious that the dumping of radioactive waste into the Irish Sea is now under investigation by the E.E.C. Commission. The Commission has the power to take the issue to the European Court of Justice. The E.E.C. Commissioner is Stanley Clinton Davis. In 1986, Mr. Davis continued to await a specialist report into the disastrous leak at the plant in 1983. He stated that if there was obvious proof of danger, the Commission would have no option but to ask for the closure of

Sellafield. Irish citizens, especially those who live on the East coast would prefer a more objective report into the operations at Sellafield. Recently, a large number of doctors from the Irish Medical Association called on the Government to demand the immediate closure of Sellafield until an international team of scientists carry out a full investigation into its safety.

Charles Haughey has again called for the closure of Sellafield, a call he first issued almost two years ago. At that time Government reaction to his call was negative and some even went so far as to accuse him of being an alarmist. Dr. Ian Paisley, leader of the Democratic Unionist Party has, in his own flamboyant style, added his voice to that of Mr. Haughey in calling for the closure of Sellafield. Gerard Brady T.D. has been a persistent critic of Sellafield over the years. He believes that the plant should be closed indefinitely. In February 1986, the Lord Mayor of Dublin, Jim Tunney T.D. called for a convention of local authority leaders on the East coast to discuss the crisis.

On 20 February 1986, a ballot by the European Parliament sought the closure of Sellafield pending a thorough investigation by experts. The very next day there was a massive leakage of radioactive material from a nuclear plant at Trawsfyndd in North-West Wales. An estimated fifteen tonnes of radioactive gas escaped into the atmosphere while the wind was blowing towards Ireland. The emission contained tritium and manganese 56. Trawsfyndd has also a history of serious accidents and leakages. It is difficult for a member of the public to understand how a huge amount of radioactive gas can escape before safety precautions are implemented. And while this book is in preparation, Sellafield continues to pump a mind boggling two million gallons of effluent into the Irish Sea. Meanwhile, we continue to lovingly watch our children at play and feed them fresh fish and shellfish from the same Irish Sea.

Margaret Thatcher has stated in her own emphatic way that Sellafield will not be shut down. Is she saying, "no closure," solely out of concern for the livelihoods of 11,000 Sellafield employees? British miners' leader Arthur Scargill might be in a position to clarify that one. In the recent past his union members got a close view of what Mrs. Thatcher thinks of the ordinary working citizen. It is significant however, that an Irish expert on nuclear technology, professor Robert Blackith, admits that Sellafield is the most likely site to produce weapons grade plutonium for Britain's new fleet of Trident nuclear missile submarines. Could that be the explanation for the secretiveness surrounding the operation at Sellafield?

Dr. George Duff, Chairman of the Nuclear Energy Board of Ireland, thinks that the four nuclear reactors at Calder Hall, Sellafield,pose a significant health risk to Ireland. The main function of the reactors is to produce plutonium as well as electricity. "A reactor has an approximate safe life span of 25 years", he added. "These reactors were commissioned in 1957 and 1959". In the recent past, there have been numerous calls for the establishment of an independent European inspectorate to monitor nuclear plants like Sellafield.

On 12 March 1986, The Report of the British House of Commons All-Party Committee on the British Nuclear Industry, was published. The Committee Chairman is the Conservative M.P., Sir Hugh Rossi. The Committee heard submissions from nuclear experts, from environmental and other interested groups and from the Norwegian Government. No submission came from the Irish Coalition Government. In fact the Labour Tanaiste, Dick Spring, told the Dail that recent leaks at Sellafield were of little significance to the Irish people. On the night of the same 12 March '86, Dail Eireann rejected a Fianna Fail motion for the immediate closure of Sellafield.

The Rossi Report makes interesting reading. It questions the continued operation of Sellafield where, according to their own investigation, there have been some 300 radioactive leaks and accidents since 1947. It criticises the amounts of radioactivity emitted and says that reprocessing should be abandoned at Sellafield. The Report states specifically that the Sellafield plant was, "the largest recorded source of radioactive discharge in the world". It concluded that the nuclear reprocessing plant at Sellafield discharges more radioactivity into the environment than any other nuclear plant in the world. The result is that the Irish Sea is the most radioactive sea in the world. It significantly states that, "the practice of discharging radioative waste into the sea on the assumption that it will dilute and disperse, works only very imperfectly." The Report chairman, Sir Hugh Rossi, concluded that there was an argument for shutting down the Sellafield plant. He urged the British authorities to immediately reduce the radioactive level of waste discharged into the Irish Sea to "zero level". The Report also criticises the amounts of radioactivity emitted and says that reprocessing should be abandoned at Sellafield. "Instead of the discharges obligingly dissipating into the ocean, they have a nasty habit of concentrating round our shores and in our seafood and coming back to us on land in a variety of ways", the Report states.

The Chairman also questioned the basis for the nuclear reprocessing operation at Sellafield. The plant produces uranium by reprocessing spent fuel rods from nuclear power stations. "It is now cheaper to buy uranium than to reprocess", Sir Hugh concluded. B.N.F. has no sophisticated methods of disposal of nuclear waste such as the use of old mines or tunnels under the sea bed. The current practice of disposing of radioactive waste at Drigg has the double disadvantage of adding unnecessarily to the volume of waste and of letting through dangerous long-lived and toxic radionuclides (radioactive particles).

"If the monitoring of the stream did one day reveal too high a level of radioactivity in the water issuing from Drigg, it is difficult to know what BNF would do about it. With nothing labelled, nothing recorded, pinpointing the offending waste would be virtually impossible. Just how haphazard the filling of the trenches appears to be is demonstrated by fires which have occurred there", the Report says.

The Committee also stated that, "we do not know enough about what happens to radioactive substances once they are released and what their long-term effects might be. It may prove in centuries to come that we have been over cautious, that the low levels we are talking about are not significant and the health consequences are negligible. Conversely, the reverse may be true and the release of even very small amounts of long-lived and dangerous radionuclides into our environment today will prove to be seriously harmful in a hundred years time when it will be too late".

The Committee also noted with grave concern, the chances of an accident at sea in the transportation of spent nuclear fuel and plutonium. The nuclear cargoes are brought from as far away as Japan. The transport ships sail near the busy English Channel and into the Irish Sea to discharge their nuclear cargoes at Barrow. The nuclear shipments are then transported by rail to Sellafield. Up to three thousand million pounds will be expended on developments at Sellafield before the end of the century. Despite many calls for its abandonment, BNF is to press ahead with the construction of THORP (Thermal Oxide Reprocessing Plant). Magnox is to be closed around 2000 AD and THORP will operate on its own. BNF optimistically predict that radiation levels will then drop to "almost zero". The Report Committee specifically urged the British Department of Energy to halt the construction of THORP if studies showed it did not warrant continuation. THORP is going ahead anyway. It is going ahead in spite of the fact that it is now cheaper to buy and stockpile uranium than to reprocess it. The Report actually states that, "given the very low price of uranium, stockpiling for many years ahead seems to be an economic alternative to reprocessing". Why then build an extremely expensive reprocessing plant? Is there a more sinister reason unknown to the public?

Meanwhile in North East Ireland, we had a presumably unintended piece of black humour. While the Sellafield debacle reached its height, Nicholas Scott, the Northern Ireland Minister with responsibility for security and defense, announced the construction of three nuclear fallout shelters. The bunkers are to be built at Omagh, Ballymena and Craigavon at a total cost of £7.8 million.

*   *   *

Before the 1986 New Year festivities were ended, Desmond O'Malley T.D. from Limerick, decided to form his own Party. He named it the Progressive Democrats. With another expelled T.D. from Fianna Fail, Mary Harney, a highly publicised tour of Ireland was undertaken. The P.D. Party captured a number of the disaffected from Fine Gael, from Labour and from Fianna Fail. They scooped up Pearse Wyse T.D. from Cork and Bobby Molloy T.D. from Galway. Amid a continuing blaze of publicity, opinion polls showed the rise and rise of Desmond O'Malley. The February '86 figures showed that opinion preferences were; Fianna Fail 42%,

P.Ds 25%, Fine Gael 23%, with Labour trailing at 4%. The shock in Fine Gael was acute. Labour was devastated. Garrett Fitzgerald was forced to hurriedly reshuffle his Cabinet. The reshuffle was controversial and riddled with denials, sackings and apologies. It was an amazing affair. Over half of the Coalition Cabinet members changed places. It was announced that two Ministers of State had resigned. They said they had not. They were then sacked by Taoiseach Fitzgerald. Barry Desmond, the Labour Minister for Health and Social Welfare, was asked to move. He refused and he lost half of his portfolio. Barry was subsequently blamed for hanging on to what he had. Gemma Hussey, a lightweight performer in Education, was demoted to Social Welfare, the former half of Barry Desmond's ministerial portfolio. By her unyielding attitude, Mrs. Hussey had precipitated the country's 40,000 teachers into strike action. It was the first teacher strike in 30 years and fears of further strikes were a serious worry to almost one million students and their parents. Her morality speech to teachers and her abrupt announcement of the closure of the modern Carysfort teacher training college, contributed directly to an enormous loss of public confidence in her ability and her suitability in Education. The reshuffle was described in the Dail by Charles Haughey as a fiasco. Fianna Fail called for a vote of no confidence in the government. Dr. Fitzgerald survived by a mere 5 votes.

By March 1986, O'Malley and the P.Ds were riding on the crest of a wave. History demonstrates however that there is always a great initial enthusiasm for something new and exciting. Quite a variety of small new parties have been registered since the foundation of the State. The more important ones are worth a glance. The National Centre party was founded in 1932 by Frank McDermott and James Dillon. In the same year the N.C.P. won 11 seats in Dail Eireann. In September 1933, the N.C.P. merged with Cumann na nGaedheal under the new name, Fine Gael. Clann na Talmhan was founded in 1938 by Michael Donnellan. In the 1943 General Election, they won 10 seats in Dail Eireann. In 1944, they dropped to 9 seats and in 1948 representation sank to 7 seats. By 1951 they were down to 6 seats and in 1954 they won only 5 seats. In 1957 they won 3 seats and in 1961, just 2 seats. Donnellan died in 1964 and Clann na Talmhan more or less died with him. Clann na Poblachta was founded in 1946. Its leader was the Nobel Prize Winner, Sean McBride. In the 1948

General Election, they won 10 seats but by 1951, their representation had dropped dramatically to two seats. In 1954 they won 4 seats and in 1957 they had dropped back to just one seat. Clann na Poblachta was disbanded soon after the 1965 General Election.

From an historical point of view, Desmond O'Malley and the Progressive Democrats could expect to win between 5 and 9 seats at the 1987 General Election. During the course of O'Malley's active political life of an estimated 20 years from 1986, the Progressive Democrats will hover for a time near 10 seats and then slowly decline into oblivion. There is the possibility that Desmond O'Malley may repeat the feat of James Dillon in 1933, i.e. he may join Fine Gael initially in Coalition and later be absorbed into the Party. Finally, he will make a personal bid to become leader of Fine Gael, perhaps in the late 1990s. Meanwhile, in March 1986, the Progressive Democrat T.Ds hold their seats in Dail Eireann on a Fianna Fail mandate.

The past vacillations of O'Malley do not augur well for his future as a party leader. When the first contraceptive legislation was introduced into Dail Eireann, O'Malley reckoned that to legalise contraceptives was tantamount to legalising fornication. He is now in favour of divorce. In the not so distant past, Desmond O'Malley made a bid for the leadership of Fianna Fail against Charles Haughey. At the crucial moment he became unnerved and backed down. What will he do when the next crucial decision arrives? Labour, the supposed Party of the Unions, went into Dail Eireann recently and voted against the arbitration award to the 40,000 strong teacher unions. A February 1986 opinion poll showed over 75% of the population rejecting Coalition Government policies. The only alternative is a speedy return to government by the largest Party in Dail Eireann.

Nearly everybody has an opinion on Charles Haughey. He is such a charismatic figure that he can never be ignored. Writing in the Irish Independent on Monday 1 April 1985, Maurice Hearne had this to say about Charles Haughey:

"In fact, I sincerely believe that Charles Haughey is one of the ablest, committed and hard-working men to have walked the Irish political stage this past quarter century. His record of achievement in four important Cabinet portfolios speaks for itself and needs no patronising confirmation from me. I believe him to be a man of superior intellect, shrewd acumen and genuine concern—a judgment that has been confirmed to me by many of the public servants who have worked with him and testified to by the host of loyal supporters he enjoys in the constituencies he has had the honour to represent."

In a wide ranging interview in the Sunday Tribune on 10 March 1985 Senator Donie Cassidy in reference to Charles Haughey said:

"There's no one to carry his case in Leinster House. There is no one to come near him as the politician supreme in parliament. I only hope that radio comes into the Dail soon, because as soon as it does, everyone will see the man that he really is, and not the man that a lot of the media portray him as. Unless he was an exceptional man, he'd never have survived, and I think that history will judge that we were very fortunate to have a leader of his class in Ireland."

POSTSCRIPT

Great heroes of legend and mythology have walked the ancient and lovely land of Ireland. We read of the Celtic warrior Cuchulainn who also features in South American Indian mythology as the deity Ku Kulcan. Ancient stories are told of Nuada of the Silver Arm, of Fionn, Oisin and the Fianna. The Sea God Manannan Mac Lir is associated with the ancient district of Seamount (Suidhe Manannan) near Malahide and Kinsaley in North County Dublin. Through the misty centuries, famous Irish men and women have etched their memory on the history of Ireland and of the world. The great Monastic Age in Ireland recalls a time when venturesome Irish priests, monks and bishops played a major role in dragging Europe out of the darker ages of ignorance, to a new era of greater enlightenment and learning.

The early 20th century saw its share of famous Irish patriots, soldiers, statesmen and literary figures. Across that stage of Irish history there strides a man whose equal has not been found or surpassed in the latter quarter of the present century. He is a fearless, hardworking, charismatic and intelligent statesman. He is consistent, forthright and compassionate in his defence of the rights of the citizens of Ireland. That man is Charles J. Haughey of Abbeville, Kinsaley.

It is this all consuming love of country and of its people that drives Charles Haughey forward to become the acknowledged leader of modern Ireland. Everything he does, everywhere he goes, every word he utters is carefully noted and analysed by the media, not only in Ireland, but far beyond these shores. Such is the all absorbing interest in Charles Haughey that, whether he is Taoiseach or Leader of the Opposition, his every move, speech and public appearance is continually relayed to a public whose fascination with the man is total.

Charles Haughey as a person and as a politician has aroused the greatest interest in the population of Ireland. He is undoubtedly the most written about and the most photographed politician in modern Ireland. He can never be ignored. He can make things happen. He is a charismatic figure and love him or hate him, one can never dismiss him. He is a journalist's dream. Thousands of column inches have been written about him. He is never petty. He has the ability to see above and beyond any situation. He forgives quickly and easily and gets on with the day's work. He has the ability to think clearly when under pressure and to make the right decisions. He is compassionate in his dealings with people. If he can solve a problem or aid a genuine cause, he will do so gladly. He is possessed of a highly organised brain with an attention to detail that is astonishing. He has a great capacity for work. A permanently relaxed person, he can draw on hidden energy long after tiredness overtakes his aides. He drives himself to the limit. He finds it difficult to tolerate time wasting or foolish talk. He mixes regularly with the ordinary people of Ireland. He knows them, appreciates their ways of thinking and in return, he is much appreciated.

He brings to Irish politics a flair and a liveliness that has been sadly lacking for many years. He has effectively turned the tide of American opinion in Ireland's favour. More Americans than ever before agree with Mr. Haughey's conception of an Ireland for the Irish people, self-governing and totally independent. Americans know the value of true freedom, of democratic self-government, of the pioneering spirit that has made the United States the most powerful nation on earth. Respected Irish-American leaders are logically and justifiably in favour of a democratic self-governing island of Ireland. President Reagan has given to Americans a new respect and pride in themselves, largely lost during the disastrous Iranian hostage crisis of the Carter administration.The time has come for a similar exercise to be carried out in Ireland. The morale of the people is at an all time low. Unemployment is high and emigration is on the increase. The summer of 1985 was the worst in living memory. Towards the end of that summer, many people began to notice paranormal phenomena in the vicinity of statues located in the Irish countryside. Thousands took to prayer in open fields by day and by night. The people needed something to divert their minds from the despair and the sadness and the new poverty creeping across Ireland.

The early months of 1986 have witnessed some dramatic scenes in Irish political life. We watched in disbelief as the drama unfolded and the burden of taxation and penury continued to suck the very life blood of our nation. We stood and waited while Minister after Minister announced the closure of establishment after establishment. Irish Shipping, half a dozen hospitals, a modern teacher training college all suffered the arbitrary flick of a finger. Thousands of business enterprises have succumbed and unemployment is rampant in every part of the land. Over 1000 million extra pounds have been borrowed since 1983. What is there to show for it? Unemployment figures have reached an all time high. Emigration has recommenced on a large scale. Those who still have a job have seen their earning power eroded. Others have endured the hardship of strikes to obtain justice.

The uncaring years of Coalition government must draw to a close. The time is also over for selfish little individuals in Fianna Fail who try to put themselves before their Party and country. They should face reality. The reality faced by the ordinary citizen of Ireland who has seen and felt his living standards drop drastically since the advent of Coalition government.

History has shown that at a time of extreme crisis in a nation's life, there appears a great charismatic leader who is ready to save his country, no matter what the cost to himself. The leader must have a single-minded determination to carry out the awesome task. He must inspire the people to lift themselves up, to believe in themselves once again and to go forward with confidence. He must be a mature, confident and compassionate figure who, by his proven ability to overcome all the odds, will inspire others to do likewise. The time is right in Ireland for the appearance of a leader who can inspire the people to help themselves. There is such a leader to boost that morale, to encourage and foster once again that pride in ourselves as an independent and viable nation. He is the only man who has the proven experience, capability and charisma to steer the Irish Republic out of its present state of depression and financial misery.

107

He is the only one with the respect, ability and power to push the Irish nation forward on the the path to recovery. He is totally devoted to the task and he will succeed. The story of Charles J. Haughey has been one of enterprise and success. The culmination of his successful life to date will be the turn-around of this small nation to the path of future successful development and self-determination. Then the dawn of a new and better era for the Irish people will have begun.

APPENDIX

DE VALERA'S REPLY TO CHURCHILL, 16 MAY 1945

Go mbeannaí Dia dhíbh, a cháirde Gael. Is libhse, a Ghaelgeoirí, is ceart dom an chéad fhocal a rá. Tá an cogadh san Eoraip caite. Ba é deonú Dé, as méid A mhór-thrócaire, sinn a shábháil ar an troid agus ar an dóirteadh fola agus sinn a chaomhnadh ar an bhfulang atá ag céasadh furmhór tíortha na hEorpa le cúig bhliana anuas.

Níor tháinigeamar slán ó cruatan ar ndóigh—is fada fairsing a theigheas droch-iarsmaí cogaidh. Ach, nuair a chuimhnímid ar na tíortha agus ar na daoine go léir mór-thimpeall orainn, is ceart dúinn ár mbuíochas croí a ghabháil go dílisdúthrachtach le Dia na Glóire as ucht sinn a chaomhnadh in am an gháibh.

An uair ba mhó a bhí an chontúirt ag bagairt orainn, d'iarras oraibhse, a Ghaela, seasamh sa mbearna bhaoil chun an náisiún a chaomhnadh. Bhí a fhios agam go mbeadh fonn ar na Gaeilgeoirí, na daoine is fearr a thuigeas céard is bríagus beatha don náisiúntacht, bheith ar tosach i measc na bhfear a bheadh ina sciath cosanta ar thír na hÉireann.

Níor chlis sibh orm, a Ghaela, Rinne sibh bhur gcion féin den obair—an obair a rinne, faoi dheonú Dé, sinn a thabhairt slán le cúig bliana anuas.

Caithfidh mé anois ionnto ar an mBéarla; tá rudaí áirithe ba mhian liom a rá agus a caithfear a rá sa teanga sin . . .

Certain newspapers have been very persistent in looking for my answer to Mr. Churchill's recent broadcast. I know the kind of answer I am expected to make. I know the answer that first springs to the lips of every man of Irish blood who heard or read that speech, no matter in what circumstances or in what part of the world he found himself.

I know the reply I would have given a quarter of a century ago. But I have deliberately decided that that is not the reply I shall make to-night. I shall strive not to be guilty of adding any fuel to the flames of hatred and passion which, if continued to be fed, promise to burn up whatever is left by the war of decent human feeling in Europe.

Allowances can be made for Mr. Churchill's statement, however unworthy, in the first flush of his victory. No such excuse could be found for me in this quieter atmosphere. There are, however, some things which it is my duty to say, some things which it is essential to say. I shall try to say them as dispassionately as I can.

Mr. Churchill makes it clear that, in certain circumstances, he would have violated our neutrality and that he would justify his action by Britain's necessity. It seems strange to me that Mr. Churchill does not see that this, if accepted, would mean that Britain's necessity would become a moral code and that when this necessity became sufficiently great, other people's rights were not to count.

It is quite true that other great Powers believe in this same code—in their own regard—and have behaved in accordance with it. That is precisely why we have the disastrous succession of wars—World War No. 1 and World War No. 2—and shall it be World War No. 3?

Surely Mr. Churchill must see that if his contention be admitted in our regard, a like justification can be framed for similar acts of aggression elsewhere and no small nation adjoining a great Power could ever hope to be permitted to go its own way in peace.

It is indeed, hard for the strong to be just to the weak. But acting justly always has its rewards. By resisting his temptation in this instance, Mr. Churchill, instead of adding another horrid chapter to the already bloodstained record of relations between England and this country, has advanced the cause of international morality an important step.

As far as the people of these two islands are concerned, it may, perhaps, mark a fresh beginning towards the realisation of that mutual comprehension to which Mr.Churchill has referred and for which he has prayed and for which, I hope, he will not merely pray but work also, as did his predecessor who will yet, I believe, find the

110

honoured place in British history which is due to him, as certainly he will find it in any fair record of the relations between Britain and ourselves.

That Mr. Churchill should be irritated when our neutrality stood in the way of what he thought he vitally needed, I understand, but that he or any thinking person in Britain or elsewhere should fail to see the reason for our neutrality, I find it hard to conceive.

I would like to put a hypothetical question—it is a question I have put to many Englishmen since the last war. Suppose Germany had won the war, had invaded and occupied England, and that after a long lapse of time and many bitter struggles, he was finally brought to acquiesce in admitting England's right to freedom, and let England go, but not the whole of England, all but, let us say, the six southern counties.

These six southern counties, those, let us suppose, commanding the entrance to the narrow seas, Germany had singled out and insisted on holding herself with a view to weakening England as a whole, and maintaining the security of her own communications through the Straits of Dover.

Let us suppose, further, that after all this had happened, Germany was engaged in a great war in which she could show that she was on the side of the freedom of a number of small nations. Would Mr. Churchill, as an Englishman who believed that his own nation had as good a right to freedom as any other, not freedom for a part merely, but freedom for the whole—would he, whilst Germany still maintained the partition of his country and occupied six counties of it, would he lead this partitioned England to join with Germany in a crusade? I do not think Mr. Churchill would.

Would he think the people of partitioned England an object of shame if they stood neutral in such circumstances? I do not think Mr. Churchill would.

Mr. Churchill is proud of Britain's stand alone, after France had fallen and before America entered the war.

Could he not find in his heart the generosity to acknowledge that there is a small nation that stood alone not for one year or two, but for several hundred years against aggression; that endured spoliations, famines, massacres in endless succession; that was clubbed many times into insensibility, but that each time on

111

returning consciousness, took up the fight anew; a small nation that could never be got to accept defeat and has never surrendered her soul?

Mr. Churchill is justly proud of his nation's perseverance against heavy odds. But we in this island are still prouder of our people's perseverance for freedom through all the centuries. We of our time have played our part in that perseverance, and we have pledged ourselves to the dead generations who have preserved intact for us this glorious heritage, that we too will strive to be faithful to the end, and pass on this tradition unblemished.

Many a time in the past there appeared little hope, except that hope to which Mr. Churchill referred, that by standing fast, a time would come when, to quote his own words, 'the tyrant would make some ghastly mistake which would alter the whole balance of the struggle.'

I sincerely trust, however, that it is not thus our ultimate unity and freedom will be achieved, though as a younger man I confess I prayed even for that, and indeed at times saw no other.

In later years, I have had a vision of a nobler and better ending, better for both our people and for the future of mankind. For that I have now been long working. I regret that it is not to this nobler purpose that Mr. Churchill is lending his hand rather than, by the abuse of a people who have done him no wrong, trying to find in a crisis like the present, excuse for continuing the injustice of the mutilation of our country.

I sincerely hope that Mr. Churchill has not deliberately chosen the latter course but if he had, however regretfully we may say it, we can only say, be it so.

Meanwhile, even as a partitioned small nation, we shall go on and strive to play our part in the world, continue unswervingly to work for the cause of true freedom and for peace and understanding between all nations.

As a community which has been mercifully spared from all the major sufferings as well as from the blinding hates and rancours engendered by the present war, we shall endeavour to tender thanks to God by playing a Christian part in helping, so far as a small nation can, to bind up some of the gaping wounds of suffering humanity.

Agus anois, caithfidh mé slán a fhagáil agaibh. Nuair a bhíos ag caint libh i dtús an chogaidh, chuíreas an tír agus a munitir faoi choimirce Dé agus a Mháthar Muire, agus is é mo ghuí anocht: Go raibh an choimrí cumhachtach chéanna oraibh san aimsir atá romhainn!

(Irish Press, 17 May 1945).

GLOSSARY

Aras: Residence.

Aras an Uachtarain: The (official) residence of the President of Ireland.

Uachtarain na hEireann: The President of Ireland.

Dail Eireann: The Parliament of Ireland.

T.D.:   Teachta Dala, a Deputy to Dail Eireann.

Taoiseach: Prime Minister.

Tanaiste: Deputy Prime Minister.

Eire: Ancient Celtic name for Ireland, derived from the Celtic Goddess Eiru. Article 4 of the Constitution of Ireland states: Eire is ainm don Stat no, sa Sacs-Bhearla, Ireland. The name of the State is Eire, or in the English language, Ireland.

Curie: The amount of any radioactive material that produces 37 thousand million (3.7×10^{10}) nuclear disintegrations per second.

Heraldic Terms

Arms: The particular family emblems or charges borne upon a shield.

Crest: The crest is placed immediately above the helmet, the helmet being immediately above the shield. The crest was originally worn on the top or side of the helmet.

Supporters: Beasts, winged humans etc. who support the shield on either side.

Motto: (French, mot, a word.) A short sentence, phrase or word having a special meaning for the bearer of the arms.

Shield: The object on which the emblems or charges of heraldry are shown.

Escutcheon: Another name for the shield.

Field: The surface or space within the boundary lines of the shield.

Bordure: The border which encloses the field.

Charges: Animals, instruments, emblems and other objects in heraldry.

Tinctures: The tinctures used in heraldry are metals, colours and furs.

Quarterly: The field or charge is divided into four equal parts by two lines, one horizontal, the other perpendicular.

Semée: When the field, crest or supporter is strewn with minor charges such as crescents or fleurs-de-lis, it is said to be semée. (French, semer, to sow, to scatter, to strew.)

115

Cross crosslets fitchée: A cross with three smaller crosses on the arms and upright point.

Engrailed: A partition line is usually straight. It is said to be engrailed when it resembles a line of waves on the sea or the letter U repeated continuously.

Chief: The upper third part of the field.

Indented: A partition line which resembles the teeth of a carpenter's handsaw.

Erased: Torn from the body. A head erased has its severed neck jagged.

Cabossed.: The head of any beast looking straight forward with the neck not visible.

ppr.: Animals, trees etc. when drawn in their natural colours are termed proper or ppr.

Crined: When the beard or hair differs in tincture from the body.

Chevron: A stripe formed by two parallel lines drawn from the bottom right and the bottom left of the field and meeting pyramidically.

Rampant: Heraldic term for a beast standing erect on the hind legs.

Passant: Heraldic term for a beast in a walking position.

Chapeau: The cap of maintenance or dignity, of crimson velvet turned up with ermine.

Per: By, by means of.

Pale: The field or charge is divided into two equal parts by a perpendicular line.

Fess: The field or charge is divided into two equal parts by a horizontal line.

Counterchanged: (French, de l'un en l'autre.) It means that the field is of two tinctures, metal and colour. The charge of metal lies on the colour and the charge of colour lies on the metal.

Crown: Originally a band worn to keep the hair in place. Later it became the distinctive mark of chieftains and kings.

Mantling: The ornamental adornment of the helmet. The mantling was originally a piece of cloth draped from the top of the helmet and covering the neck and shoulders to protect the bearer from the scorching sun, particularly during the eastern crusades.

Fasces: Bundle of rods with axe in the middle carried by lictor before a high magistrate or consul. The ensigns of authority and high office. (Latin, fascis, bundle.)

Dexter: Right.

Sinister: Left.

Arg.: Silver.

Sa.: Black.

Az.: Blue.

Or.: Gold.

Gu.: Red.

Vert: Green.

Erm.: Ermine, an animal akin to a weasel and valued for its fur. In heraldry, a symbol of purity and dignity.

116